The City Project

Strategies for Smart and Wise Sustainable Urban Design

Volume 1

Series Editor

Dario Costi, Department of Engineering and Architecture, University of Parma, Parma, Italy

Editorial Board

Roberta Amirante, Department of Architecture, University of Naples Federico II, Napoli, Italy

Guya Bertelli, Department of Architecture and Urban design, Politecnico di Milano, Milan, Italy

Marko Bertogna, Department of Physics, Informatics and Mathematics, Università di Modena e Reggio Emilia, Modena, Italy

Andrea Boeri, Department of Architecture, University of Bologna, Cesena, Italy

Andrea Borsari, Department of Architecture, University of Bologna, Bologna, Italy

Nicola Braghieri, Laboratoire des Arts, École Polytechnique Fédérale de Lausa, Lausanne, Switzerland

Ali Cheshmehzangi, Department of Architecture and Built Environment, University of Nottingham, Ningbo, Zhejiang, China

Antonio D'Aloia, Dipartimento di Giurisprudenza, University of Parma, Parma, Italy

Paolo Desideri, Department of Architecture, Roma Tre University, Rome, Italy

Morena Diazzi, Knowledge Economy, Employment and Company, Bologna, Italy

Sergio Duretti, Network Department, Lepida ScpA, Bologna, Italy

Agostino Gambarotta, Department of Engineering, University of Parma, Parma, Italy

Gabriele Lelli, Department of Architecture, University of Ferrara, Ferrara, Italy

Giovanni Leoni, Department of Architecture, University of Bologna, Bologna, Italy

Francesco Leali, Engineering "Enzo Ferrari", University of Modena and Reggio Emilia, Modena, Italy

Francesco Manfredi, Management, Finance and Technology, University LUM Giuseppe Degennaro, Casamassima, Italy

Carlo Mambriani, Department of Engineering and Architecture, University of Parma, Parma, Italy

Eugenio Mangi, Department of Architecture and Built Environment, University of Nottingham Ningbo China, Ningbo, China

Roberto Menozzi, Ingegneria e Architettura, Università di Parma, Parma, Italy

Antonio Montepara, Department of Engineering and Architecture, University of Parma, Parma, Italy

Marco Mulazzani, Department of Architecture, University of Ferrara, Ferrara, Italy

Carlo Alberto Nucci, Department of Electrical, Electronic and Information, University of Bologna, Bologna, Italy

Simone Scagliarini, Department of Economics "Marco Biagi", University of Modena and Reggio Emilia, Modena, Italy

Andrea Sciascia, Department of Architecture, University of Palermo, Palermo, Italy

Annalisa Trentin, Department of Architecture, University of Bologna, Bologna, Italy

Marco Trevisan, Department Food Science and Technology, University Cattolica del Sacro Cuore, Piacenza, Italy

Dario Zaninelli, Department of Energy, Campus Bovisa, Milan, Italy

Michele Zazzi, Department of Engineering and Architecture, University of Parma, Parma, Italy

Managing Editors

Emanuele Ortolan, Department of Engineering and Architecture, University of Parma, Parma, Italy

Andrea Fanfoni, Department of Engineering and Architecture, University of Parma, Parma, Italy

The book series *The City Project* reports on applied research and operational developments that promote urban renewal and the sustainable transformation of contemporary cities. Inspired by the "City of Man" as imagined by Adriano Olivetti and Ernesto Nathan Rogers, and going beyond the concept of the smart city and related technological advances, the series' goal is to present holistic, practice-oriented and multidisciplinary strategies for realizing the City 4.0, i.e., the city of the fourth industrial revolution, in keeping with the objectives of the UN's 2030 Agenda for Sustainable Development.

In particular, the series reports on effective design, planning and management approaches that leverage urban and architectural design skills, engineering, environmental and social expertise, and administrative abilities alike. It welcomes books on each of the aspects mentioned above, as well as studies analyzing multiple aspects, their interactions and/or holistic solutions. *The City Project* addresses a very broad readership, including designers, engineers, architects, social scientists, stakeholders and public administrators, who deal with various aspects of the realization of the City 4.0. It publishes theoretical investigations into the contemporary built environment, international case studies, and pilot projects concerning urban renewal and the regeneration of urban areas, as well as the proceedings of key international conferences.

Books published in this series are devoted to supporting education, professional training and public administration. Outstanding Ph.D. theses on emerging topics, if properly reworked, may also be considered for publication. The series is published with the support of the Smart City 4.0 Sustainable LAB, an interdisciplinary teaching and research project on future cities initiated by the University of Parma, and jointly implemented with other regional universities (the University of Bologna, University of Ferrara, and University of Modena and Reggio Emilia).

About the Cover

The cover of the book series *The City Project* features a painting by Carlo Mattioli (C. Mattioli, *Estate in Versilia*, 1974, oil on canvas cm. 118 × 70, Catalog n. 1974D0029, Courtesy of Fondazione Carlo Mattioli, thanks to Anna Zaniboni Mattioli)

The horizon of poppies painted by Carlo Mattioli between the dark background of the forest and the white plane of the wheat, becomes for us, thanks to a transfiguration of meaning that aligns with the attitude towards abstraction rooted in the figure of the painter, a city which is intertwined with its landscape, evoking the idea and the possibility of recomposing a balance and seeking an integration between settlement and environment, between human space and natural element.

More information about this series at http://www.springer.com/series/16644

Dario Costi

Designing the City of People 4.0

Reflections on Strategic and Sustainable Urban Design After COVID-19 Pandemic

Dario Costi
Department of Engineering and Architecture
University of Parma
Parma, Italy

Translated by Sean Nation—CITI Traduzioni

ISSN 2730-6992　　　　　　　ISSN 2730-700X　(electronic)
The City Project
ISBN 978-3-030-76102-8　　　ISBN 978-3-030-76100-4　(eBook)
https://doi.org/10.1007/978-3-030-76100-4

© The Editor(s) (if applicable) and The Author(s), under exclusive license to Springer Nature Switzerland AG 2022
This work is subject to copyright. All rights are solely and exclusively licensed by the Publisher, whether the whole or part of the material is concerned, specifically the rights of reprinting, reuse of illustrations, recitation, broadcasting, reproduction on microfilms or in any other physical way, and transmission or information storage and retrieval, electronic adaptation, computer software, or by similar or dissimilar methodology now known or hereafter developed.
The use of general descriptive names, registered names, trademarks, service marks, etc. in this publication does not imply, even in the absence of a specific statement, that such names are exempt from the relevant protective laws and regulations and therefore free for general use.
The publisher, the authors and the editors are safe to assume that the advice and information in this book are believed to be true and accurate at the date of publication. Neither the publisher nor the authors or the editors give a warranty, expressed or implied, with respect to the material contained herein or for any errors or omissions that may have been made. The publisher remains neutral with regard to jurisdictional claims in published maps and institutional affiliations.

Cover illustration: C. Mattioli, *Estate in Versilia*, 1974, oil on canvas cm. 118 × 70, Catalog n. 1974D0029, Courtesy of Fondazione Carlo Mattioli, thanks to Anna Zaniboni Mattioli

This Springer imprint is published by the registered company Springer Nature Switzerland AG
The registered company address is: Gewerbestrasse 11, 6330 Cham, Switzerland

Preface

UNKNOWN AUTHOR, *Trionfo della Morte* [Triumph of Death], mid 15th century, Property of Galleria Regionale di Palazzo Abatellis, Palermo (authorization Prot. 3103 01.10.2020)

I wrote much of this book on the spur of the moment, during the first wave of the pandemic, almost as a release. The dates at the beginning of each paragraph mark those long weeks in which the whole world got lost, in which, all of a sudden, time seemed to stop. My diary of words, with some personal experiences of that tragic event, and the diary of images collected during those same days by Alex Majoli in Italian cities, together became a springboard for reflection on what COVID-19 has made us realise.

During this period, I developed the conviction that we must think of the coronavirus as a wake-up call, as a solicitation to act on reality to modify it, to fully exploit the enormous potential that the fourth industrial revolution—that of interconnection and interactivity—has given us, but channelling it towards an ultimate goal, which has yet to be specified.

We must first consolidate a "Culture of technology" that is still lacking today, and we must put a human soul into digital technology, re-establishing its role as a tool, while also thinking about which concept of society and, consequently, of city we want to pursue. If it is to be, as I hope, the updating of the *Città dell'uomo* (*City of Man*), as conceived by Adriano Olivetti in terms of *Community* in the post-war period (he too was facing the dawn of an industrial revolution of which he was a protagonist—the third one, which saw the discovery of the computer), then we will be able to think about how we can now improve the space of human interaction using the extraordinary tools we have.

We must therefore have the courage to transform difficulty into opportunity. It is certainly not just a question of technology. In fact, the issue we are looking at is not related to all this innovation. It is primarily a cultural issue on the basis of which we must orient our actions in a progressive direction. The pandemic has removed, at least for the moment, the veil of custom. Many worn-out conventions that we have inherited, many conflicts that seemed unresolvable, now seem nothing more than dialectics to be developed, extremes to be connected and made to interact, in order to share a decision-making strategy to knit back together with those *Communities* that today seem lost, liquefied, disintegrated.

This is the fault line along which the book you are about to read inaugurates *The City Project* Series for Springer,[1] of which it constitutes the methodological premise and the starting position. The declared goal is to discuss and share, at an international level, the very feasible possibility of regenerating contemporary cities together with their inhabitants, through the urban project, intended as a tool for interpreting the many skills that are interested in it and the equally numerous experiences that deal with it.

Its original title, preserved in the Italian edition, was *Diario Manifesto per la Città delle Persone 4.0*, designed to make an explicit connection between the individual experience of the pandemic and the collective and civil commitment to the consequent transformation of settlement. The title was designed to stimulate the reader's empathy by connecting his/her personal microcosm to the collective macrocosm. Sometime later, however, we

---

[1] See *The City Project* Series on the *Springer*'s website at https://www.springer.com/series/16644.

decided to remove—in the English language version—some emphasis from that definition to make the message less personal and more operational, to make it more accessible and to stimulate a debate as broad as possible, thanks to the series we are inaugurating. In fact, a few months have passed since the time of writing the book. I am writing this preface in the so-called second wave, as the first vaccines are already being administered. The book will be released shortly, when perhaps it is all over or is about to be. In the meantime, the conditioning of COVID-19 is becoming a rule, the limitations are marking our habits and certain forced gestures are becoming part of our daily life.

Locked down in my study under self-isolation, my thoughts turn to the future. I think of 2021 as the space for possible action rather than an unconscious return to the former reality.

The question we must ask ourselves is: what will happen when COVID-19 is no longer a threat?

Maybe we can and should imagine this scenario. I am afraid that we will be faced with the materialisation of two obvious parallel and complementary risks: finding ourselves suffering for years from the effects of this experience of deprivation in our behaviour, while at the same time forgetting the lessons we have learned, removing the bereavement from our minds once the problem has been overcome. Both of these attitudes are humanly understandable, but must be carefully avoided, especially in their likely combination.

Instead, we must immediately react to this probable double drift. The only remedy I can imagine is a critical jolt, still possible today thanks to the emotion of the moment, a declared acquisition of awareness that only public debate and civil society can determine. If, from today, we are able to collectively reflect on what has happened, tomorrow we will be able to value the lessons that the epidemic has left us.

We will be able to take advantage of this global tragic event if we take the opportunity to rearrange the urban space around people and allow them to interact in a way that has not happened for decades.

Then, in a few years, we will really be able to look back on the 2020 pandemic as the epiphany that revealed the shortcomings of the city to everyone and forced them to identify the strategies to reconfigure the places we live, rediscovering long-lost habits and focussing on what we realise are our current needs, which we can finally address with relevant solutions.

Parma, Italy
December 2020
(During the second wave)

Dario Costi

Acknowledgements

What Is Not Seen

A book is always the tip of an iceberg rising out of the sea. There is much more ice supporting it under the water than we can see above the surface. Likewise, this work is a small part of a very large and complex structure. It is the last layer of years of research and studies on cities for which I have to thank the group of the University of Parma, with Emanuele and Andrea at the forefront. It relies on the consistency of the collective reflection initiated by the research laboratory on the contemporary city—Smart City 4.0 sustainable LAB—which we are promoting along with many colleagues from the universities of Emilia Romagna, thanks to essential contributions from Carlo, Michele, Francesco, Giovanni and Marco.

The text emerged in a matter of weeks precisely because it was firmly grounded on the sedimentation of years spent reflecting on strategic urban design with many administrators throughout Italy, also thanks to the continuously renewed impetus from Francesco and Alessandra. Once drafted, it was pushed along last few metres with loving attention by Leontina. The book moves, like a block of ice following the ocean's currents, in a clear direction of civic commitment that I adopted by instinct and absorbed from my upbringing, that I assimilated from the air I breathed at home since childhood. For this, I have to thank my parents.

But how does this great mass of ice keep from sinking? The iceberg stays afloat thanks to a light yet sturdy core that pushes it up from below. For me, that core is the luminous heart of the matter, namely Simona, Alessandro, Antonio and Andrea.

Introduction

A. Majoli, *Italy, Syracuse. March 24, 2020. Italy has recorded about 68.000 cases of infected people and 6800 deaths.* © Photo: Alex Majoli/Magnum

The City of People Project 4.0

Are we already forgetting?
Fortunately, the worst seems to be over. The curve is on a steep decline, even though the health emergency remains painfully present. In Italy, things are going much better but people are still dying. Fewer every day, but they are still dying. Meanwhile, infection continues to spread in most parts of the world.
A few weeks into Phase 2, a dangerous yet understandable psychological dynamic is spreading around us: the systematic removal of the tragic and universal experience of coronavirus.
We know that shutting problems out is the first reaction, a spontaneous response to overcome difficult moments in life. We know that denial is the immediate solution, the most instinctive but also the most superficial reaction. We will only be able to transcend this collective suffering by further analysis of the trauma we have undergone. Only by developing a shared reflection will we be able to process our grief and put this event behind us without leaving an unresolved memory.
Yesterday, today and tomorrow are all part of the same process. Reflecting on what has happened is important and not only to avoid hiding from this experience. It is an issue we need to face for two reasons that we can link together. It is a necessary condition for providing rapid responses to the immediate needs of the health emergency but, much more importantly, it is also an opportunity if we take a slightly longer view. It is the opportunity to reorder human settlement and to reorganise contemporary cities in the light of the problems we have had to face and thanks to the potential we have glimpsed, through individual and collective reflection. The shock of these past few months has provided the greatest stimulus to start working on our cities. This turn of events has demonstrated the need for extraordinary commitment and the importance of taking back control of the urban form through the urban project.
These circumstances have provided me with the reason and the opportunity to write this book. Launching an international series of publications on the city project at this time means adopting a particular stance that sees this moment in history both as a revelation and as an opportunity. I, therefore, designed this *issue zero* as a manifesto of themes and a declaration of intent. I thought it might be useful to start by outlining the basic issues to be tackled and with a synthetic and strategic reflection on the contemporary city driven by the health emergency. *The City Project* series of books that we have been planning since last year aims, in fact, to ignite a debate on applied research in the international scientific context and on operational developments that promote urban regeneration and the sustainable transformation of contemporary cities in the era of the *Fourth Industrial Revolution*, centred on the people who inhabit them. The series is inspired by the idea of the *City of Man* that was developed by the enlightened entrepreneur Adriano Olivetti and

pursued by the architect Ernesto Nathan Rogers in the post-war period.[2] By refining, clarifying and in some ways surpassing the still rather uncertain and multiform concept of smart city that we have inherited, this editorial effort seeks to present the many strategies and contributions that humanistic culture and scientific culture can bring together in realising the *City 4.0*—the *City of People in the fourth industrial revolution*—in line with the objectives of the United Nations Agenda 2030 for Sustainable Development. Precisely because of the project-oriented and practical nature of the approach we want to develop, I imagined that the first few issues of the *Series* might outline the scenario and guide future actions. This initial release is therefore a cultural preamble to the work that awaits us.

Following on from these general considerations, the next step is to clarify the content of this book and the dialectical intent of the text, which is both a diary and a manifesto. Some background is therefore necessary. I have little faith in the immediate and sometimes haphazard responses to emergencies, or in off-the-cuff musings by architects seeking visibility. I believe much more in taking time to reach decisions on settlement issues and in an aware and informed future, in the lesson of history that we should try to pursue, with the aim of building up a new *Culture of Technology* as the necessary operational framework for our time. For these reasons, I have kept a pandemic diary and noted down the links between this truly bizarre event in our lives, the problems of the contemporary city that we have investigated from the outset and the practical prospects for its regeneration that we are now studying. This *Phenomenological Diary*[3] that I am presenting links the emotions, experiences and revelations of this difficult and painful period with ongoing research, perhaps all too directly. It strengthens the convictions that drive our commitment in the fields of project-based research, recommending that they be shared as widely as possible.

What happened in the first few months of this year has opened many people's eyes to the problems we are facing. It brought many related issues to light: the neglect of the city, the difficulties faced by communities and the needs of society. It created a necessity for things that were already for the most part ready and available. In fact, we are living a moment in history that could resolve inherited conflicts through the positive development of certain dialectics that began to emerge in the early months of 2020.

---

[2]See the debate popularised in Italy in the post-war years, on the line between philosophy and architecture, starting from Olivetti's model of civil commitment for the construction of a *Concrete Community* of individuals in A. OLIVETTI, *La città dell'uomo*, Op. Cit. Rogers uses the definition of *The City of Man* in E. N. ROGERS, *Il Cuore: problema umano delle città* in *Il cuore della città*, edited by E. N. ROGERS, J. L. SERT, J. TYRWHITT, Milan 1954, Records of CIAM Bergamo 1949, pp. 72 and 73. *The City of Man* was recently the subtitle of the international architecture magazine DOMUS during the editorship of Nicola Di Battista from 2013 to 2017.

[3]I use this term to indicate the approach that has guided our research and projects for some time. To some extent, it references the crossover between phenomenological philosophy and the modern movement that I consider the distinctive root of Italian architectural culture. This approach envisions the project in the urban environment of greatest interest, which has been neglected for far too long. The definition obviously refers to E. PACI, *Diario fenomenologico*, Milan, Bompiani, 1973.

In examining the phenomena with which we have long been familiar through the lens of the epidemic, we will be able to interpret them for what they really are. We will see that some of these conflicts can now be resolved: the conflict between the inertia we were used to and the trauma we have experienced, the reconcilable conflict between tradition and innovation, the primarily unconscious conflict between people and the space they inhabit, the still obligatory conflict between body and environment, the static conflict between home and work, the conflict between large and small settlements, the increasingly less redundant conflict between communication and information, the conflict we need to eliminate between form and substance, the conflict between development and form of the periphery that needs to be rehabilitated through the project, and the conflict we can no longer escape between governance of processes and projects in progress.

If we are to transform the difficulties into opportunities, we must resolve the dualities that we have seen rather surprisingly coming closer together in recent months. We need to reflect on interactions such as identity/society, community/city, vitality/community, domesticity/mobility, activity/interactivity, truth/connectivity, frugality/contemporaneousness, reality/project orientation and private/public. From these interactions, we can obtain a new perspective built on the foundations of ancient customs.

By confronting them, a number of strategic actions may emerge that we can implement one after the other. REACT, RESUME, LIVE, MOVE, INHABIT, SERVE, UNDERSTAND, THRIVE, CHANGE, ACT: in my view, this is a feasible agenda of commitments for the coming years. They form a sequence of keywords that could be translated into a work programme. They are the foundations for a debate across the various fields of knowledge in order to initiate a project-oriented approach and good practices for our immediate future. This will then allow us to reflect on what has happened in a fruitful and positive way, despite everything. This is the only way that we will be able to interpret the problem as a stimulus to fully exploit the capacity we are consolidating as we go through this tragic interlude. We will see that many of these relationships hark back to forgotten practices from the past that can be revived and updated using modern technologies. In doing so, we will enjoy that pleasant feeling of reviving old habits, which served us well and for which we have at least some nostalgia, using new tools and with a new awareness.

If we can generate a high-level critical debate, then past and future can interact to overcome problems that seemed insurmountable until recently. We will realise what the virtual amplification of reality demonstrates: that innovation can actually be key to rediscovering identities. This will allow us to recover the true meaning of the term *tradition*, which Rogers himself reminded us is linked through its root to the concepts of both *translation* and *betrayal*,[4] underlining how the transmission of identity always passes through development and openness to obsolescence.

This must be our approach in facing the problems and the opportunities presented by this moment in history. The fear provoked by 2020 can then become an opportunity not to be wasted. The dramatic reminder of the importance of urban coexistence and the new intensity focussing our actions once more on public health can be channelled simultaneously towards a transformation on two fronts: the transformation of our settlements into wise and intelligent cities that are viable because they are sustainable, and the transformation of our lives into a critical experience that leads us to forge closer ties with those around us.

This perspective, which needs to be described, discussed and shared could also be the starting point for a radical mobilisation of the population. This could in turn lead to a real renewal of both *urbs* and *civitas*, of the city of stones and the city of people, as the economist Stefano Zamagni always reminds us.

Parma, Italy

June 2020 (During the first wave)

The City of Man will arise in a world liberated from subjugation to the unbridled power of money, when the struggle in material and spiritual realms that has been the overriding commitment and purpose of my life has finally been laid to rest. As my father often told me, the light of truth shines out through deeds alone and not through words.

So what should we do? What is the responsibility of urban planning against this stark picture, increasingly tragic according to daily reports and even to the most optimistic of temperaments? We must dig down with determination into the secret dynamic of the third industrial revolution and push forward courageously with bolder plans.

In Italy, we are witnessing widespread positive economic and technical phenomena, whose effects in the material, cultural and spiritual domains could be sterile, or could instead bring forth a new type of civilisation. It depends on how well we understand the most profound and sensitive phenomena that, following an inscrutable design, condition both human greatness and human wretchedness.

A. OLIVETTI, *Città dell'uomo* [The City of Man], first edition 1960, republished for Edizioni di Comunità, Ivrea 2015. The first sentence is taken from the back cover, while the second is contained in the speech *Urbanistica e libertà locali* [Urban Planning and Local Freedoms] on p. 80

The ultimate goal is to emphasise the ways in which technology and society can coexist. We should not see the former as an exogenous force over which we have no control. We do not have to choose between living with or without technology. Instead, we should see the incredible change taking place as an

---

[4]E. N. ROGERS, *La tradizione dell'architettura moderna, conferenza inaugurale della Settimana dell'architettura, Trieste June 1955* republished in *Architettura, misura e grandezza dell'uomo, Scritti 1930–1969* Vol. II edited by S. MAFIOLETTI, Il Poligrafo Padova 2010, pp. 555–561.

invitation to reflect on who we are and on our worldview. The more we stop to think about how to manage this technological revolution, the more we will analyse ourselves and the social models that these technologies represent and favour, and the more opportunities there will be for this revolution to improve society.

K. Schwab, *La quarta rivoluzione industriale* [The fourth industrial revolution], Franco Angeli, Milano 2016, p.16

Contents

1 **How Covid-19 Has Opened Our Eyes** 1
   1.1 From the Conflict "Inertia Versus Trauma" to the
        Transformation of Difficulties into Opportunities 1
   1.2 From the Conflict "Tradition Versus Innovation" to the
        Collective Identity of the Society of the Fourth Industrial
        Revolution 4

2 **How People Experience the City** 9
   2.1 From the Conflict "People Versus Space" to the Place
        of the Community in the City........................ 9
   2.2 From the Conflict "Body Versus Environment" to the
        Vitality of Convenience 12

3 **How People Experience Their Home and the Public Spaces**... 17
   3.1 From the Conflict "Home Versus Work" to the Connection
        Between Domesticity and Mobility.................... 17
   3.2 From the Conflict "Big Versus Small" to the Dialectic
        Between Activity and Interactivity 21

4 **How Human Languages Change** 25
   4.1 From the Conflict "Communication Versus Information"
        to the Truth of Connectivity......................... 25
   4.2 From the Conflict "Form Versus Substance" to the
        Frugality of Contemporaneity 28

5 **How Improve Our Real-World Settings**................... 31
   5.1 From the Conflict "Development Versus Form" to the
        Forward Thinking Starting from the Settlement Reality 31
   5.2 From the Conflict "Governance Versus Commitment" to
        the Emulative Dialectic Between Private and Public....... 35

How Covid-19 Has Opened Our Eyes

1.1 From the Conflict "Inertia Versus Trauma" to the Transformation of Difficulties into Opportunities

REACT

11.03.2020_But what on earth has happened? The whole world has changed in the last two weeks. I think back to the workshop at the end of February spent with students around the drawing boards. I am thinking about David, who may have caught it, but he's doing OK. I am thinking about last Sunday's training and lunch with the under 13 s. Thankfully the quarantine period is over. It's been 14 days since those last moments spent with the others and nothing has happened to us yet. I counted them one by one. The symptoms we were waiting for never arrived. Fortunately. I'm truly relieved, and not just for myself. It means they are all fine too. Waiting for the virus to strike and the defences we have put up are changing perceptions of what we have done, what we had been doing and what we can do in the future. Everything has stopped. Everything around us is on hold. Or perhaps not. Something is stirring, however …

In a recent webinar with young entrepreneurs, I explained how employment has been in a permanent state of crisis for many years, how recent generations have become used to difficulties as the norm. For them, the health emergency is just the latest in a series of difficulties they have had to overcome, only this time the bar is set higher. Many of them have changed how they work and have edged their companies towards more advanced, more evolved, more competitive positions. Before going any further, we should explore the original meaning of this term. «*Crisis*» from the Greek $\kappa\rho\sigma\iota\varsigma$ means *choice, decision, decisive stage of an illness* and comes from the verb $\kappa\rho\nu\omega$ which, in turn, means *to distinguish, to judge*. Therefore, the primary meaning of crisis is choice. But not just any choice. A choice that can lead to overcoming a serious difficulty and to healing. Today's negative meaning would seem to be a mere nuance in the original context. The original meaning was more related to responsibility and the need to decide. That is exactly what it means today as well. All these recent events present us with the necessity but also with the opportunity to make individual and collective decisions, to make important if not decisive choices.

In 2020 we have lived through one of those moments where everything comes to the surface. Throughout history, unexpected accidents and extraordinary conditions have sometimes triggered paradigm shifts, sped up the sluggish pace of momentous change and led to real-world adoption of models that had been waiting in the wings but had not been considered seriously until that moment.

Fig. 1.1 A. MAJOLI, Italy. Catania. Sicily. April 1, 2020. At the cemetery. All funerals have been suspended. © Photo: Alex Majoli/Magnum

Let us hope then that the fear of the last few months and the worries over another epidemic appearing sooner or later will encourage us to look further ahead than usual. Let us hope that this is the right opportunity to embark on a far-reaching process of reflection on city living and to launch concrete processes for its physical regeneration. If we look back again for a moment, before focusing on the goals we can set ourselves, we will find many of these issues reappearing like foam on the long waves of history, like the possible and necessary re-emergence of issues returning in various forms to the surface, of problems put on hold, of dynamics moving faster than our pace.

Urged on by the unexpected return of a widespread spirit of sharing and unforeseeable rediscovery of humanity, we must set ourselves the goal of combining the extraordinary civil tradition of life in European cities with the great innovations of our age that can bring it up to date.

In the middle of this pandemic, the historian Alessandro Barbero considered how plagues have always had *unforeseen consequences*.[1] He reminded us that reactions to dramatic events such as these have produced substantial changes in approach, with positive structural effects. After the Antonine Plague at the end of the Second Century, the Roman Empire did not replace the lost labour with new slaves by launching military campaigns to conquer distant lands. It did just the opposite. Instead, it

---

[1] *Conseguenze inattese. Su come l'umanità reagisce alle catastrofi* [Unexpected consequences: how humanity reacts to disasters] was the title of his inaugural lecture at the 2020 Virtual Book Fair in Turin held on 13.05.2020 at the Mole Antonelliana, which is still available on the Book Fair's Facebook page. My thanks to Antonio D'Aloia for pointing this out.

placed new value on human capital and for the first time opened up to foreigners who wanted to come in. Similar positive repercussions also emerged after the Black Death, when the structural response was an increase in wages and the implicit recognition of the importance of workers. This all demonstrates that the current problem can become an opportunity if we react properly and respond to the trauma with good decisions. We must remember, however, that cultural transformations are neither automatic nor guaranteed. Although humanity has always shown an extraordinary capacity to react, the will to change is the necessary condition for these tragic events to be transformed into social improvement.

Epidemics are therefore an opportunity to *change the world*.[2] This was stated by philosopher Laurent de Sutter during the weeks of *lockdown*, who rediscovered the Greek meaning of the word ἐπιδήμος—literally a force *threatening the people*—as a rite related to the appearance of the gods. In antiquity, epidemics were ceremonies and sacrifices offered to the gods, but also to foreign powers whose arrival in the city could represent either a serious threat or an extraordinary opportunity. In reflecting on the paradox that the virus has spread around the world thanks to the increasingly efficient infrastructures developed by humankind, it becomes clear that to overcome the problem we need to think globally about how to build another world, with different balances and a newfound capacity to allow differences to coexist.

I too see the emergence of this virus as a break with our previous life. I think it should be grasped as a great opportunity to bring about radical reorganisation of cities, including through coordinated and strategic initiatives. We must, therefore, exploit this dramatic event and build on what we have learnt. Separation from friends and family ties that we had taken for granted, the absence of the public space that we had neglected, first-hand experience of the narrow confines our homes and the inadequacy of our cities are all lessons that we can put to good use. The need to cooperate and share, the necessities imposed by social distancing, the awareness of having to use our homes for more than eating and sleeping and being forced to rethink how we get around the city as individuals are just some of the stimuli that can motivate us to reassess how we live. If properly addressed, these issues can map out an alternative scenario to the reality we have inherited.

It is like being in the dressing room after a first half spent chasing the other team around the pitch. We can switch from the man-to-man marking and continuous shadowing forced upon us by a bad tactical strategy to a proactive approach that transforms the counter-attack into a turnaround on the field. This will require a team reaction. We can set up an effective offensive play if we act collectively as a unit. While catching our breath at half time, if we decide to correct the approach that has blighted the championship so far, we can come back and win this match, but we can also establish the right approach for future games. We will then be able to change the direction of this season and climb back up the league table. If we think of these first few months as time out—a necessary pause to reorganise the game—if we can use the time that we have for deeper reflection, beyond the necessity of overcoming this health emergency, we can rearrange the game plan and reorganise the attack. Putting aside this metaphor, we can now look carefully at things that we have had in front of us for a long time but that we could not see. We will be able to reconcile many conflicts that seemed insurmountable. We will then realise that overcoming this latest difficulty could end up settling differences that seemed irreconcilable.

Starting from the transformation of the difficulty into an opportunity, we can then establish some dialectics through which we can analyse the revealing dynamics of the first few months of 2020. Doing this not only lets us try to interpret what has taken place, but also enables us to imagine a new start based on good habits of old that have been rediscovered, supplemented and extended by the

---

[2] L. DE SUTTER, *Cambiare il mondo, l'epidemia e gli dèi*, TLON Rome 2020.

virtual word. We will understand that, once we get beyond the most immediate simplifications, the increasingly accessible new technologies—if they are channelled properly—may well be the decisive tools for re-imagining urban culture through the new awareness that the epidemic has forced upon us. We will then be able to reorganise the next few years based on the values we have reclaimed and on the scenarios we can share.

1.2 From the Conflict "Tradition Versus Innovation" to the Collective Identity of the Society of the Fourth Industrial Revolution

RESUME

22.03.2020_Every day is the same during lockdown. My body moves around the house from memory, almost automatically, with no unexpected events to resolve or appointments to attend. As in the iconic film "Groundhog Day", the alarm clock and movements around the house are now always the same. I got up early again today without even realising it was Sunday. I look through my WhatsApp chats. Mauro from Milan sends me a link to visit the Brera art gallery from my sofa. Francesca in Parma regularly shares paintings and watercolours from a beautiful collection that we have never visited, even though it's right on our doorstep. Today she is describing the nineteenth century painting "Calesse con musicisti in piazza di paese" [Carriage with musicians in the town square]. This is an opportunity to see what the church square of Santa Croce was like and to understand how people experienced this location two centuries ago. She points out the band of musicians, the children in the street, the carriage with the coachman, the fashion of the era with its top hats, canes and ankle boots.

The debate in recent decades has become fixated on a number of epic conflicts that have tormented us for a long time as if they were intrinsic natural laws. Local versus global and tradition versus innovation are just two of the cultural conventions that we had absorbed as motifs of the era in which we were living. Although these issues reflect truly central contemporary questions, opposing reactions have in the meanwhile grown up around them and transformed them into stereotypes that can be exploited. As a result, alternative models, pockets of denial and environments of conflict have emerged. These are all matters that we took for granted, but are we really convinced they are all true?

In light of what has happened, I think we should now be asking another question. Are we sure that all these conflicting concepts are irreconcilably opposed?

The background to these polarisations that impede any possibility of synthesis and any reasonable shared progress is the seemingly inevitable conflict between old and new, between before and after. Now, also thanks to Covid-19, perhaps this head-on collision can be avoided and we can try to bridge the gaps between past and future, which are too far apart today. An in-depth examination can then reconnect many issues seen until now as irreconcilable alternatives and imbue them with positive meaning.

But let's start at the beginning. The way we inhabit our homes and cities is the historical result of ancient settlements common to all peoples, expressed in each particular context according to the specifics of geography, climate, conditions and events. As we know, the leaps by which human activity has surged forward during this long collective process of maturation are reflected most enduringly in historical cities and urban monuments as testimony to a repetitive and ever-changing

Fig. 1.2 A. MAJOLI, *Italy, Palermo. March 21, 2020. The statue of Santa Rosalia at the entrance to the chapel on Mount Pellegrino.* © Photo: Alex Majoli/Magnum

idea of city.[3] Their civil and identitary significance—as Rogers reminds us again,[4] in Latin, *monument* has the same root as *memory* (*memini*) but also as *warning* (*moneo*)—are constructed testimonies through which all citizens recognise themselves in a shared sense of belonging. They are the cornerstones selected by time and by the people around whom the city has gradually taken shape, the symbols that aggregate its community. They are a presence that requires a collective commitment to continuation.

The settlement is therefore the result—constructed using the technology available at any given period—of a continuously renewed social contract and of progressively stratified cultural development. These long-term dynamics encounter epoch-defining transitions and changes that trigger paradigm shifts and sudden accelerations in increasingly tighter succession. As the humanities remind

---

[3] J. RYKWERT, *L'idea di città, Antropologia della forma urbana nel mondo antico* [The idea of city, Anthropology of the urban form in the ancient world], 1963 recently republished in Italy by Adelphi Milan 2002.

[4] E.N.ROGERS, *Gli elementi del fenomeno architettonico* [The elements of the architectural phenomenon], Christian Marinotti Edizioni, Milan 2006 p. 73.

us, perhaps the first of these fundamental changes—the one that oriented the Western worldview from left to right—was the change between Homer and Thucydides, the transition from *myth* to *writing* that set the narrative in a rational and transmissible framework, laying down a codified interpretation of the Western world. We have understood that this transition not only determined the layout of the pages of the books we read, the exhibition trails in museums and the sequence of information we pick up visually. It has also affected how we think, how we act and how we see things.[5]

Once again, something is now happening that may change how we see the world. As in those origins, we are once again witnessing a reorganisation of the logical space of our minds, with clear future repercussions on physical space too. For some years now, we have been talking about *brainframes*,[6] the visual space for relating to the virtual interface to which our brains are adapting, stimulated constantly by text and images on digital devices. At the moment it is difficult to assess the neurological and anthropological impact of this new habit to which we have all succumbed. Therefore, we need to figure out what is happening. Of course, we need to understand its limits, but we also need to realise its potential. This is a situation that we cannot avoid but, precisely because of this, it is also an opportunity on which we need to reflect carefully. We will then discover that this situation, which has been forced upon us, may also open up a new opportunity for a many-sided debate to be consciously exploited. The sociological point of view would hope for responsible activation of a *connective intelligence* capable of transforming this new situation in which we have suddenly found ourselves into an open space for permanent interaction between individual perspectives. We must therefore ask ourselves how our way of interpreting things will change, how we can reshape the cultural identity in which we have grown up and what the critical foundations of the society we can build may look like.

While today we are taking our first steps in remodelling our way of thinking, we must also realise that this current situation is also the last stage of a rapid transformation of the technical possibilities developed by Western civilisation.

Just as writing changed our approach in ancient times, other moments have gradually changed the rules of engagement of human life on earth. Among all the changes that have informed our complex way of conceiving and using physical space, technological revolutions have undoubtedly played a leading role. The recurring dialectic between these structural innovations, society, cities and architecture is a defining chain of influences that has led to great changes and many advantages. It has, to a large extent, also shaped—although not always for the better—the legacy of our experience of the world. We know that the *Fourth Industrial Revolution*[7] through which we are living began almost without our realising it just over a decade ago. If we think about it, the *smartphone*—the tip of the iceberg and iconic symbol of this new dynamic that is changing our lives—arrived in Italy very recently, only around 2010. As we all know, the key features of this latest leap in innovation are facilitated interactivity and permanent interconnection. Behavioural consequences are already visible and have quickly become a widespread way of living, without any cultural preparation or mediation. We are still only at the early stages of a radical change in social behaviour and we are faced with two interlinked situations: we can see some immediate and worrying tendencies, but we can also glimpse ways of collective virtual interaction that have encouraging and largely unexplored potential.

How should we deal with this unexpected and so far rather unconscious change? How can we control its impact on a society silently overwhelmed by this revolution and, consequently, on the city where that society lives?

---

[5]D. DE KERCKHOVE, *L'architettura dell'intelligenza* [The architecture of intelligence], Testo & Immagine, Turin 2001.
[6]D. DE KERCKHOVE, *Brainframes, Mente tecnologia, mercato* [Brainframes, Technological Mind, Marketplace], Baskerville, Bologna 1993.
[7]K. SCHWAB, *La quarta rivoluzione industriale*, Op. Cit.

Without wishing to disappoint, I don't think anyone has the answers to these momentous questions yet. Perhaps all we can do is identify some protective antibodies, devise some positive approaches to this dynamic and invoke a collective process of critical reflection. If we look around, we will realise that we are not the first generation to face such issues. If we examine the reactions to previous industrial revolutions, we can in fact recognise ourselves in the militant experiences and cultural battles of our ancestors. We are aware of the strong link and common philosophical outlook[8] between the *civilisation of machines* and Le Corbusier's *machine for living in*, but also the remodelling of living space that he imagined, based on the life of man liberated in his relationship with the landscape, defined in the architecture/manifesto of the *Esprit Nouveau* pavilion.[9] We are also familiar with the critical approach that permeated fields of knowledge and areas of reflection in the early decades of the twentieth century. About a hundred years ago, faced with the effects of the Second Industrial Revolution, the European cultural avant-garde was already clear about the importance of modernity, but also about the danger of the uncontrolled rise of the primacy of technology. Historians, philosophers and intellectuals like Ernest Bloch and Walter Benjamin as well as representatives of all the artistic fields—writers and poets like Paul Scheerbart, painters like Paul Klee, architects like Adolf Loos—preceded us in these concerns.[10] All of them felt the need for a formal reduction imposed by the times during which they lived. They all feared the loss of the cultural legacy they had inherited.

Today we are all living in this same state of concern as we face an even greater power of technology. The *Angelus Novus* painted by Klee and described by Benjamin is today still the symbol of this condition of suspension between yesterday and tomorrow. Let's reread his words: *There's a painting by Klee called 'Angelus Novus'. It depicts an angel who seems to be moving away from something on which his gaze is fixed. His eyes are wide open, his mouth is open, his wings are outstretched. This is how the angel of history must appear. His face is turned towards the past. Where we see a chain of events, he sees one long catastrophe relentlessly piling up ruins and tipping them over at his feet. He would actually like to stay behind, awaken the dead and rebuild the ruins. But a storm is blowing down from heaven, it gets caught up in his wings and it is so strong that he can no longer close them. This storm overwhelms him and pushes him into the future, against which he turns his back as the heap of ruins rises before him into the sky. This storm is what we call progress.*[11] Like him, we too are now in the middle of two opposing currents. One is propelling us forward towards the future and the other is pulling us back towards the past, which we keep in sight, though somewhat disoriented, trying not to lose our bearings and our identity.

We must respond to this fear with a feeling of trust that can become a commitment to work. During those same years, with the help of theologian Romano Guardini, the architect Mies van der Rohe sought an answer through his work. Therefore, echoing the words from the 1920s means relaunching the cultural as well as the civil commitment of critical modernity in the contemporary world, projecting it onto even further horizons: *Far from reducing technology, we need to increase it. Or rather: what is needed is a stronger, more measured, more "humane" technology. We need more science,*

---

[8] An enlightening reflection on these themes, pointed out to me by Giovanni Fraziano, was explored philosophically in P. STOLTERDIJK, *Sfere III, Schiume*, Raffaello Cortina Editore, Milan 2015.

[9] The project and rebuilding of the Pavilion was recently reconstructed on the occasion of its restoration in *Phoenix, il padiglione de L'esprit Nouveau tra ricostruzione e restauro*, edited by M. B. BETTAZZI, J. GRESLERI and P. LIPPARINI with expert advice from G. GRESLERI, LiberAmicorum, Bologna 2018.

[10] W. BENJAMIN, *Karl Kraus* (1931), in *O. C.*, vol. IV, Einaudi Turin 2002, p. 357: *The inhuman stands among us as the messenger of a more real humanism. […] One needs to have already followed Loos' struggle with the "ornament" dragon, to have heard the astral Esperanto of Scheerbart's creatures or glimpsed Klee's "new angel"—who would rather liberate men by taking away what they have than make them happy by giving—in order to understand a humanity that asserts itself in destruction.*

[11] W. BENJAMIN, *Sul concetto di storia* (1940), in *O. C.*, vol. VII p. 487.

but it must be spiritualised, more subject to the discipline of form; we need more economic and political energy, but it must be more evolved, more mature, more aware of its responsibilities...[12]

About thirty years later, in the transition between the second and third industrial revolution, one of its earliest pioneers, Adriano Olivetti, had the same concern and felt the same need for a critical and spiritual foundation to the dynamic that he saw taking place and that he was to some extent shaping as a protagonist. His words are very clear: *A mortal danger is looming over us because the modern world where mechanisation has taken charge could overwhelm real man with all his integral value.*[13]

The issue we have before us today, as we face the *Fourth Industrial Revolution,* is still the same one. How can we achieve a more *humane* technology today? Looking ahead to issues that will be explored in the following pages, we can in the meantime note Guardini's suggestion to stimulate the development of more evolved and more mature economy and politics, while recovering the spiritual dimension our past. We will see later that a major development in this direction has already been underway for a few years and that Covid 19 is perhaps an opportunity to support and affirm this process in the context of a new social contract between public and private. In any case, focussing on issues like these means realising that we are facing a radical paradigm shift and that the best strategy for us is to build our future approaches, enhanced by new technologies, on the great cultural tradition that we carry with us and on the contemporary awareness that we can share.

Therefore, the opportunity of a digital revolution also means the necessity for cultural resistance.

Everything may be ready to contribute in defining what the society of our era—the imminent *Society 4.0*—will be. The memory of accumulated historical behaviours that shaped settlement and that had been forgotten in recent decades has been reawakened from the sleep of *quarantine*. The tools to make them viable again, also on the wider scale of the peripheries yet to be configured, are now available. The emergency that has triggered this convergence may—if we can channel its impact effectively—produce extremely important outcomes for our community and, as a result, for our cities.

Cities 4.0.

---

[12]R. GUARDINI, *Lettere dal Lago di Como, La tecnica e l'uomo* (1923–1925), published in 1927, in Italia Editrice Morcelliana Brescia 1959, edition consulted 2013, p. 98.

[13]A. OLIVETTI, in *La città dell'uomo*, Op. Cit.

How People Experience the City

2.1 From the Conflict "People Versus Space" to the Place of the Community in the City

LIVE

25.03.2020_*I arrived early to avoid a long wait. The shopping centre car park has been reconfigured as a queue snaking its way between the parking bays out to the road. There is a queue for shopping at any time of day. Perhaps because masks or gloves are making it hard to use their smartphones, people are looking up and around. I say hello to Luciana. She's sorry the initiative planned by her voluntary association has been postponed. There on the pavement I meet a guy called Sandro. He asks me about the electric car I have just left recharging. We talk for a bit about the right distance. In any case we've got time to kill as we move forward together. It has become a rare occurrence to stop and talk to people you meet by chance. I'm almost inside. A lady reminds me that we can also do shopping for people who are not able. We can leave whatever products we like with her on the way out. I'm about to go in. I look back and I wonder: what if there was a square or a garden instead of all that tarmac?*

Besides the conflicts we have listed so far, many other differences can perhaps be reconciled if we make the most of this opportunity. One of these has remained quite hidden and tacitly accepted for a long time. This is the conflict between people and the space in which they live.

A few years ago, at a round table of proposals for *Parma Città Futura*, my colleague, a lecturer in paediatrics, pointed out that the primary cause of the explosion in childhood obesity is the so-called environmental issue, i.e. the fact that children do not have a welcoming city outside their front door where they can meet others and get physical exercise in a community setting, like they always used to do.[1] A few minutes later, a geriatrician confirmed the problem, wishing for a pleasant space to keep the elderly moving too by creating a network of public parks closer to where they live. It might be hard to believe, but if we think about it, that really is the situation. The neighbourhoods in our suburbs are a social problem to the point of being a health risk, and not only for the most vulnerable groups. Very few, apart from those of us who are trying to change things and the specialists who study the problems of children and the elderly, were even aware of the issue. The experience of Covid-19 has now brought many of these problems to the fore. Having them highlighted is therefore an extraordinary opportunity that we never imagined having even a few months ago. The most worrying thing

---

[1] The proposals of the ten thematic tables, including the one on health and well-being, are collected in *Parma Città Futura Volume II. Il libro bianco* edited by D. Costi, MUP Editore, Parma 2017.

Fig. 2.1 A. MAJOLI, *Italy, Catania. March 14, 2020. In the city center.* © Photo: Alex Majoli/Magnum

is that this system of settlement and the model for living that it determines are not even perceived as a necessary evil. They are just accepted as a given. However obvious it may be, everyone has been living the recent city as normality, even though we know that settlement in recent decades is instead the result of complex processes that have developed without recognising the central importance of people and by and large avoiding real project-oriented thinking. It is the space to which man has adapted, the place to which he has become necessarily attached following a natural survival instinct, despite its harshness and shortcomings. The inadequacy of the contemporary city is therefore an issue that was hurriedly consolidated in recent decades and that is only coming to light now because of the health emergency.

We now need to state clearly that the pandemic has exposed many shortcomings: the city, in its current form, is not only incapable of defending us against the virus. It is simply inhospitable. It removes opportunities for social interaction and denies the physical conditions for the community to maintain and renew itself.

I often recall the simple yet disarming question that Francisco Barata asked us a few years ago at a conference on the relationship between *Social housing and the City*:[2] *everyone talks about the right to housing, as they should, but why does no one ever talk about the right to the city*?

I addressed this theme—*the right to the city*—when I spoke about *Smart Cities* at the conference held in late 2019 on *New technologies and the future of public law* in a discussion with legal

---

[2]*Casa pubblica e città. Esperienze europee, ricerche e sperimentazioni progettuali*, edited by D. COSTI, MUP Monte Parma 2009. Compare with H. LEFEBVRE, *Il diritto alla città*, Marsilio editori, Padova 1970.

philosophers, computer engineers and constitutional experts.[3] With some deliberate simplification, I drew comparisons on that occasion between the *Charter for Human Rights* in 1945 and the *UN Agenda 2030* of 2015, calling for a debate on the highly urban relevance of this increasingly global challenge. I still didn't know that during those months, on the very eve of the pandemic, that *Elogio della città* [*In Praise of the City*] by jurist Giovanni Maria Flick had been published. Among the many standpoints from which he interprets the reality of settlements, I was struck by the legal consistency of this proposition that I, as an architect, had merely suspected. His interpretation associates the city with the concept of *social formation* debated by the Italian Constituent Assembly. In so doing, he raises the question—now more topical than ever—of responding to a right enshrined in the Charter, given that *social formations are a place and an instrument in which and through which the individual expresses his or her personality.*[4] The city, in this legal interpretation, is therefore an instrument for implementing individual rights enshrined in the Italian Constitution.

If this is the case, it will then be important to reopen a debate on the right (also constitutional) to the city and to try to find a viable answer. Perhaps this is exactly the right moment. In this case too, Covid-19 marks a break with old conventions. Faced with challenges to civil coexistence and the endangering of many people's lives, perhaps we are now in a position to ask the question, in order to develop a strategic vision of the city that we want and to find the strength to pursue it. After the drama we are still experiencing, an extraordinary commitment to truth and mobilisation will be required. However, this is not just a technical or administrative matter for specialists to debate. It is also a major cultural and collective issue that must be shared with the population. From this perspective, the fear of the virus has stimulated an immediate reaction that must be recognised for its vigour. The pandemic has brought out a rather touching humanity to which we had grown unaccustomed. One of the few positive results to emerge from this dramatic period is undoubtedly the widespread mobilisation that has sprung up spontaneously everywhere. The fact that we have all felt a collective fragility, if only for a few months, has plunged us into a precarious condition like we have never experienced before. We have all been the *silent army* fighting this war, to use a religious turn of phrase.[5] *An army whose only weapons are solidarity, hope and a sense of community that have re-emerged in these times when no one can survive on their own.* For a few months, the *social poets* of the peripheries were all the citizens who, regardless of their background, found themselves in the role of volunteers reacting to the unexpected difficulties of this period. These are all those people who rolled up their sleeves to protect and help their families, their neighbours and parts of the social system, whom everyone has encountered and supported, even through small everyday gestures.

Therefore, the great legacy that this pandemic will leave us is above all the awareness of a strength that we no longer thought we had. The reaction to being faced with a problem that we cannot solve on our own becomes a great opportunity for everyone.

The *liquid modernity* described worryingly by Bauman as the *consumer society*[6] that has loosened social ties through a highly individualistic approach may perhaps coagulate once again thanks to these renewed human reactions and the rediscovery of relationships with others. We now need to reflect on

---

[3]*Le nuove tecnologie e il futuro del diritto pubblico*, Florence 22–23 November 2019, ICON-S Italian Chapter. I took part in the panel discussion *Constitutional rights in the age of smart mobility: problems and perspectives* chaired by Simone Scagliarini.

[4]G. M. FLICK, *Elogio della città? Dal luogo delle paure alla comunità della gioia*, Paoline Milan 2019, p. 68.

[5]These are the words addressed by Pope Francis to the popular movements around the world. See the collection of letters in Pope Francis, *Life after the Pandemic*, Libreria editrice vaticana, Vatican City 2020. The following quotation is taken from p. 37.

[6]Z. BAUMAN *Modernità liquida*, Laterza, Bari 2002. An updated perspective is captured in the short interview *Futuro liquido, Società, uomo, politica e filosofia* edited by E. PALESE, Edizioni AlboVersorio, Milan 2014. See the paragraph *Il futuro della società* pp. 29–36.

how this vitality can be maintained and how to avoid losing the momentum built up over the last few months. If our rediscovered civil commitment can continue even after our isolation and fear, we can then launch an open debate on how to improve the space in which we live.

Human relationships have in fact always been the bedrock of cities, at least until a few decades ago. In the post-war period, people still discussed it as a strong yet sensitive concept. The philosopher Enzo Paci and the architect Ernesto Nathan Rogers discussed this with the aim of shaping post-war *Reconstruction* through architecture—thanks to the constructive dialogue between phenomenology and modern project development—as *a node of relations, a focal point of the relationship.*[7]

So that is the point from which we must restart: from the social and cultural project of building spaces for a community of individuals, of setting up places that will welcome people's experiences so that they can poetically inhabit the city where they live. This may be the right time to start again based on ancient principles, to resume that approach and reinvigorate that line of argument that has never really been discussed and developed in depth.

We must therefore underscore this point clearly and reiterate a number of related concepts.

Over the last few weeks, we have been thinking about how to make the most of this unforeseen historical event. Many are suggesting that we should not go back to yesterday's world. Many are asking for a general rethink of the way we live together. Some imagine re-establishing a leading role for civil society, for those communities of people who have in recent decades lost faith in a shared commitment. The real challenge facing contemporary society is, therefore, to channel this positive drive of today into areas of discussion on the future. The possibility of asserting this *right to the city* that no one had ever claimed before could emerge from this convergence. This city where we live—interrupted, incomplete and in many ways just wrong—needs to be retuned, according to the *idea of city* that we can imagine as a community, to the wavelength of our rediscovered desire to invest our energies. We can therefore ask ourselves how we can finally begin transforming the settlements where we live, starting, for once, from the suburbs. Once again, we can affirm that the pandemic has served some purpose if the interlude of *quarantine* has opened our eyes to possibilities that we had previously overlooked. The difficulties of a recovery create the conditions for a truly incisive intervention, if we can just imagine it and implement it not only as an emergency response but also as an opportunity for targeted remodelling. We only need to make small but essential changes that will satisfy this newfound eagerness to get involved and the willingness embraced by many to find a new way of living in the physical space we have discovered, different to the approach we were used to … and which we thought the only possible way until recently.

2.2 From the Conflict "Body Versus Environment" to the Vitality of Convenience

MOVE

01.04.2020_Axel is seven and he can't wait to get back to the Cittadella, his favourite park. It's not that far from the apartment where he lives, but he has understood that people cannot go there, at least for a while. He goes out onto the balcony and scans the skyline to locate it. He thinks he can see it in the distance through the apartment blocks. The playing fields enclosed by the Farnese walls have been his mirage in these last few months. He dreams of meeting up with his friends and racing around the amusements and fields, and up the earthen mounds. He besieges the ramparts in his nightly dreams. On the way to the shops he persuades his dad to take him to the moat so he can

---

[7]E. Paci, *Il cuore della città*, in Casabella-Continuità 202, 1954, pp. VII –X (presentation of the book *Il Cuore della città* edited by E. N. Rogers, J. L. Sert, J. Tyrwhitt, Milan 1954, CIAM Bergamo 1949).

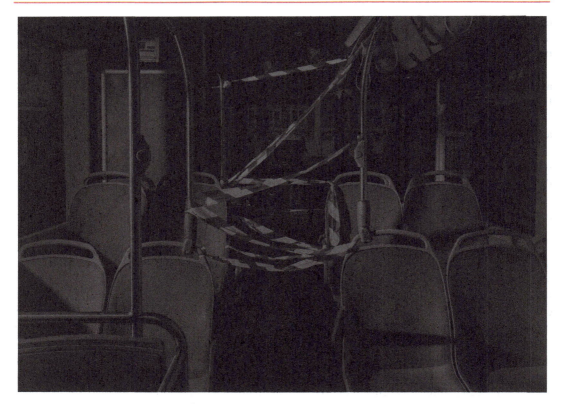

Fig. 2.2 A. MAJOLI, *Italy, Catania. March 19, 2020. Public transport has been cut to 50% from their daily schedule, drivers are trying to protect themselves from the travelers.* © Photo: Alex Majoli/Magnum

look at it from outside. His mother Camilla does the shopping, but now she does it every day, unlike before when she did it once a week. She goes out and walks to the shops further away in the city centre. In any case, she'll be back again tomorrow and the daily shopping is always fresh and light to carry. Meanwhile, just outside the city, Stefania can't resist the temptation and takes the dog out for a walk, a bit too often. Sometimes they go further than the legal limit to get to the riverbank for their walk. She strays a bit too far and risks getting a fine.

For several years now, growing sensitivity to environmental issues and healthy lifestyles has made more and more people interested in physical exercise. It has made people more open to cycling and walking and has challenged the concept of maximising comfort through sedentary activities and motorised transport.

Today, more than ever before, comfort means being able to move freely in pleasant and protected surroundings. Reimagining the city as a hospitable place is therefore the first raising of awareness that we must put to good use. The effects of interrupting human activities encourage a pause for reflection and some possible changes. The return of animals to the streets and ports, the contemplative rediscovery of nature and clean air have been the immediate effects of this interruption of people's lives. We will soon discover whether fine particles really do help the spread of the virus, which could give us hope for cleaner air, thereby achieving an historic result that statistics on respiratory diseases, health scares and legal limits have not managed to achieve so far.

However, we can see immediately that we will need to change our habits if we are to maintain these obvious rediscoveries at least to some degree. If we take a big breath now, making the most of the clean air that will soon become polluted again, and reflect deeply on what these signals tell us, we will easily realise that a radical reflection on how we live and where we live will be necessary.

We just need to think of how people have been meeting in the streets and visited each other, albeit at a safe distance, rediscovering opportunities for controlled personal relationships, even in queues outside shops. Therefore it should come as no surprise that freed from cars the streets have once again welcomed people waiting to go shopping, demonstrating the obvious fact that under safe conditions, everyone is happy to get around by walking and cycling. We will finally realise that if they have not done this before, it was not out of laziness but due the lack of a welcoming space designed for individual movement to be a pleasant experience rather than a risk.

When things get moving again soon, cities will need to have figured out what to do. They must have realised the need to rethink urban traffic, prioritising slow mobility for its obvious advantage of being individual and, as such, not a vehicle of infection.

In late April 2020, the mayor of Milan,[8] looking ahead to the reopening after *lockdown* had put the country on hold for two months, asked for government funding to mark out bicycle lanes on the roadways and to facilitate the purchase of personal electric transport equipment. In mid-May, the mayor of Brussels announced a 20 km/hour speed limit for the entire historic centre. Pedestrians and cyclists will finally have priority over motorists.[9]

In these, and in many other cases, the remedy of social distancing to combat transmission of the virus in social gatherings would seem to be the prime motivator in getting cities to reassess how their inhabitants move around. The administrators of all communities around the world must be reminded that, once this emergency is over, they cannot lower their guard, because other pandemics may occur and repeat the tragedy of the last few months.

We must therefore remind not only them but all of us that the time has come to change the way we use collective land and that getting around the city on foot or by bicycle will not only be a way to avoid infection and defend ourselves against the virus, but also an opportunity for social experience, like life in urban settlements was for centuries. Historically, people have not only transited but also inhabited spaces—houses, but also the city—according to a broad principle of usage that is not only physical, but also perceptive, emotional, sentimental, intellectual and cultural. Body and mind are immersed daily in surroundings that influence actions and thoughts, for better or for worse.[10] The experience of our daily movements means much more than simply getting from A to B. In fact, getting around also means embarking on a process of continuous discovery of people and places that come face to face often unexpectedly, through chance meetings with others and timely coincidences. Each experience changes us based on what happens. Possible contacts, different times of day and the different environmental conditions of the seasons make the space we pass through both changeable and stimulating. Furthermore, let's not forget that living in the city has always meant appreciating the unexpected, drawing inspiration and pleasure from unexpected encounters. If we recover the richness of this urban culture of the chance meeting, we will be able to reimagine settlements not simply by criss-crossing them with new cycling paths for moving people around but instead by the progressive implementation of a system of places to welcome those people as they move around. We will therefore need to think about linking up city parks to create a sequence of green spaces to reinforce

---

[8]https://milano.corriere.it/notizie/cronaca/20_aprile_29/nuova-mobilita-milano-23-chilometri-nuove-piste-ciclabili-65e336f2-8a17-11ea-94d3-9879860c12b6.shtml?refresh_ce-cp.

[9]https://it.euronews.com/2020/05/01/sindaco-di-bruxelles-e-il-momento-di-cambiare-piu-piste-ciclabili-in-citta-milano-close.

[10]For a reflection on this topic, between phenomenology and contemporary architecture see G. Böme, *Atmospheric architectures. The aesthetics of felt spaces*, Bloomsbury, London 2017 and P. Zumthor, *Atmosfere. Ambienti architettonici. Le cose che ci circondano*. Electa Milan 2007.

and encourage people's willingness to move independently, by giving them a safe and comfortable environment in which to do so.

The vitality that has been so severely limited by quarantine therefore signals a civil and social opportunity to make the public city hospitable and comfortable, as well as practicable. In substance, this requires strategic interventions to sew the whole urban landscape back together for collective uses and to make it available for the rediscovered need to reclaim the streets.

Rethinking the contemporary city now means first and foremost developing the vision of an *accessible and welcoming green city*. The first step in this direction is to stop making the mistakes that many have made. The first of these is undoubtedly creating cycle paths wherever possible. This nearly always means along the pavements next to the roads, at least in Italy. Since this priority has now become obvious to everyone, we must make it clear that a different approach is crucial. We must make it clear that slow links across the city must not be simply infrastructure for travelling at a slower pace alongside existing roads. This proximity, with the dangers and the smog it entails, instead of encouraging actually hinders a voluntary transition to the slow-paced individual mobility that many would be willing to embrace under optimal conditions. We must therefore create green links between the existing parks in order to provide a system of public spaces across the city as an ecological, economic and social background to our everyday journeys in the not too distant future, while providing a concrete and practical demonstration of sustainability. The consolidated experiences of many cities in northern Europe highlight the success of this alternative structural approach. Much is already in place in our country too, and I can assure you that it is much simpler than it may seem.

Essentially, we need to think about making the episodic nature of our weekend leisure time a permanent and everyday feature of our lives. To do this, we need to establish structural conditions so that the exception of immersion in nature becomes the norm for all city dwellers as they go about their daily business, with obvious advantages in terms of reducing pollution and consumption, increasing physical activity and the safety of places frequented by people. As we have shown, in many contexts a few strategic interventions will suffice to incorporate urban green spaces into a new alternative system for individual travel as well as for personal experiences.

3. How People Experience Their Home and the Public Spaces

3.1 From the Conflict "Home Versus Work" to the Connection Between Domesticity and Mobility

INHABIT

08.04.2020_Next week we will have the first online degrees from our university. We accepted them with some reluctance. For more than a month, we have had remote sessions for undergraduates. All I can do is help them from home. They are here with me on my computer screen in the living room. Meanwhile, Fabio is trying to get hold of me to discuss the project we are developing remotely. He asks me how to resolve that detail of the entrance. I take a break and manage to sketch a view of it and send it back to him with my smartphone. Meanwhile Diletta continues. He asks me for a few more minutes to check the table of contents of his thesis and to improve the tables again. We go over it again. In any case, I'm already at home and we still have some time to continue. I walk around in the daylight of the garden, listening to him on my laptop. I remember the darkness of the ring road a few months ago. The rhythm of a typical day has disappeared. The children are no longer waiting outside the changing rooms to be picked up. In one way, I miss it, but I am also at least a bit relieved. We go over everything again, we can still improve the work.

One of the great unresolved issues of contemporary urban life is how to reconcile leisure with work commitments. The challenging relationship between home and work has until now meant the painful obligation of travelling at fixed times over fixed distances, repeated day in, day out. This is an issue that has never been confronted and has become the norm, accepted by everyone. A rule of life that has consumed so many things for decades: life, time, energy, petrol, oxygen. Two months' suspension has highlighted this waste that we had taken for granted. *Lockdown* has been a test that has yielded encouraging results through the environmental and social reflections prompted by *smart working*. A survey of the Italian Public Administration[1] records that 73.6% of employees have worked from home and that the simple fact of not travelling to the workplace has resulted in many personal and collective savings. These can be summarised with some impressive figures: an average of 1.5 h/day of travel per person, 1.75 tons of PM 10 particles and a total of 8000 tons of carbon dioxide.

These figures call for a deep reflection on the traditional dynamics between home and work that we had taken for granted. During these months, we have all realised that many of our movements are not that necessary. We have realised that it can be much more efficient and less complicated to work without having to leave home at least a few days a week. While the approach of urban design for

---

[1] https://www.enea.it/it/seguici/pubblicazioni/edizioni-enea/2020/il-tempo-dello-smart-working.

Fig. 3.1 A. MAJOLI, *Palagonia. Sicily. April 3, 2020. Dr. Elena Lomita from Catania ASP (provincial health agency) visiting patients in their homes to test Covid-19.* © Photo: Alex Majoli/Magnum

vacant land can stimulate new ways of individual, ecological, healthy and social travel, the underlying necessity of moving around must also be completely rethought. Work on vacant collective urban spaces as discussed in the previous pages must be matched by work on occupied individual residential spaces. The forgotten potential of the home must therefore be recovered. In fact, we must also completely rethink the living space, not just because we might find ourselves confined to it on future occasions, but also because it could be pleasant and comfortable to make our living space productive and interactive. The great era of energy regeneration and seismic securing of buildings, which began some time ago and has now been relaunched with promising tax incentives—in Italy as much as 110% of the costs will be offset in the coming years as advance taxes—must therefore also include remodelling the existing collective housing stock to rediscover the memory of that fertile mixture of functions of the historic city and the flexible use of space that it guaranteed. The concept of housing as construction of a space for sensitivity and empathy, with its extraordinary potential to bestow (or deny) happiness, can once again become the focus of design research, starting from this new need, which we will see is actually an old need, to accommodate the various moments of the day. We can start again from the great settlement tradition of the domestic space as the centuries-old combination of environments modelled around people's lives, moulded to fit the needs of the various times of day and structured according to the traditional relationship between the indoors and the outdoors.

As the architect Andrea Sciascia reminded us during the cycle of interdisciplinary seminars *Stare nella Distanza* [Keeping a distance], organised in Naples to explore possible responses to Covid-19, there are some projects of the Modern Movement which, in contrast to the indifferent affirmation of technology at that time and about a hundred years before the emergency we are facing now, indicate the route we still need to travel in rethinking the space for living.[2] He reminded us of the value—now more current than ever, when faced with the problems posed by the pandemic—of those projects envisioned by Le Corbusier with the collective dwellings of the *Immeuble Villas* transformed into a system of family units overlooking the landscape and separated by green terraces, or the Mies court houses that subdivide the vacant land as private gardens. In both cases the relationship between indoor and outdoor space is the focus of a residential reflection in which the project reinterprets age-old traditions. In fact, these proposals are not futuristic inventions that appear out of the blue. As often happens also in cultural transformations, especially in the most sensitive and profound instances, they become transfigurations through which the memory of people's lives resurfaces. If we look for precedents for these projects, we will discover that the first one recalls the monastic settlements of Italian Carthusian monasteries and that the second one reinvents the residential logic of the Roman patio house in the fluid space of a modern dwelling in the midst of nature.

We can then revisit and develop the discarded examples that in turn update models refined by history. By recovering the principles that guide these design experiments in their anthropological depth, we can launch a widespread action of residential remodelling that can be activated and propagated, starting from social housing and public housing. With a view to reducing journeys between home and work, while encouraging the rediscovery of a social and community dimension in neighbourhoods, we can combine *smart working* policies focussed on individual homes with a parallel strategy of increasing *co-working* spaces in the suburbs. In many abandoned contexts or in underused buildings we can then promote the reactivation of existing structures to create collective spaces open to the public, occupying the latest urban fabrics with the economic and productive fabrics that inhabit them. Among the other opportunities for settlement, the ground floors of public residential stock, on which work is to be carried out as part of the seismic and energy regeneration programs, may be an ideal location to consider in light of their upcoming availability. Many shared areas and garages on the ground floors of these buildings will be affected by necessary structural work and could be transformed into local workspaces, and not just for residents.[3] Adapting individual houses and shared spaces in city districts for the permanent presence of people therefore means putting the structural conditions in place for a collateral dynamic also in the field of mobility. Implementing a coordinated strategy to relocate houses reorganised for *smart working* and places equipped for *co-working* to the periphery can therefore significantly reduce urban travel, with positive side effects not only on people's lives but also on public mobility.

In this context, the reduction of personal needs and the truly viable alternative of a system of parks and protected public spaces for crossing the city on foot or by bicycle could be accompanied by a radical change in the nature of motorised traffic. While the transition from combustion to electric vehicles is becoming increasingly popular, promising a progressive reduction in pollution, another further change will completely transform the very concept of the car. In fact, we are close to an epoch-defining revolution that will transform how cars are seen, from an object to be owned to a service to be shared.

Self-driving is now almost ready to transform ownership into a service and vehicular transport into a need to be met on demand. The promised scenario is surprising. As far as we can predict today, the

---

[2] I am referring to the lesson entitled *Nuove tecnologie, architettura, città e paesaggio* [New technologies, city and landscape] given by Andrea Sciascia at the review *Stare nella distanza* [Keeping a distance] organised remotely by Francesco Rispoli to deal with these issues on 22 May 2020 from the Federico II University of Naples. See http://www.diarc.unina.it/index.php/42-importanti/2402-ciclo-di-seminari-stare-nella-distanza.

[3] To this end we are developing *Guidelines for a sustainable strategy for regeneration of housing stock on an architectural, residential and urban scale in the relationship between social housing and the city* as part of the ongoing research for the Unicapi Residents' Cooperative in Modena.

prospects are certainly interesting. The numbers we are talking about are astonishing (but still to be verified). The target of 80% LESS—an 80% reduction in parking space required, 80% reduction in accidents, 80% reduction in pollution—will make this transition extraordinarily persuasive and convincing. Combined with the spread of electric transport, the advent of its application could trigger an important domino effect of interlinked virtuous dynamics: opening a historical scenario of environmental regeneration, drastically reducing the time and cost of individual travel, while freeing up large sections of areas currently occupied by parked cars and making them available to people.

Let's imagine then that the transformation of roads into cycling/walking paths, currently improvised as an immediate response to the health emergency, may be interpreted, to use a medical metaphor, as an intervention necessary to save the patient. Once the acute crisis we are experiencing has passed, we will have to take steps to treat the patient with the attention she deserves and with the time necessary: after keeping her in *Intensive Care* as long as it takes to save her life, we will then have to move her to *General Medicine* to carry out a full anamnesis and make an accurate diagnosis, before creating a rehabilitation plan. This is the only way we can allow her to make a full recovery, make sure she is well in the future and avoid other life-threatening episodes. What we are seeing today must therefore make us reflect extensively on the appropriate therapy for the real illness of modern-day cities. If we think about it, the symptoms of the malaise had already been present for some time: shops closing down, smog getting into houses, a horizon of cars parked for weeks on end, the difficulties of getting around and the time wasted looking for a parking space. All these situations that we have accepted as normal are the signs of the loss of the central role of people and the disappearance of the tradition of social living that previous generations enjoyed. They are signals that Public Administrations can no longer underestimate or pretend not to see. This serious difficulty we are facing today indicates the need to structure a strategic systemic response that goes beyond the acute phase. It must plan the therapy, start the treatment and monitor compliance—as doctors and pharmacists refer to checking that their instructions are followed over time—until health that has been compromised for so long is finally restored.

All this now seems necessary. Today's problem confirms the huge potential of rearranging urban parks as a system of locations to be crossed, on which we insist so much as part of the Strategic Urban Design methodology. We then need to see whether this new strategy of protected urban relationships can be integrated with such a significant recovery of urban land as that offered by self-driving vehicles. What could we achieve if we could imagine transforming 80% of the existing car parks into green and public space? It would certainly be an opportunity to rearrange empty urban spaces for pedestrian and bicycle traffic while at the same time an opportunity to revitalise the high street. In such a scenario, shops could once again do a bustling trade with all those people moving around the city on a daily basis. Staying with the abstract for a moment—although later on everything will have to be examined concretely and in light of the particularities of each urban situation—let us imagine recovering not only the huge areas currently dedicated to parking, but also the rows of parking spaces that line our roads as green pathways. Our city roadways could be accompanied by a strip of equipped park which, together with the existing footpath, could pave the way for a revolutionary reorganisation of public space. The cycle and pedestrian paths along pavements could be replaced by linear green squares with an environmental but also a commercial value. We could have usable sections of even 10 m to be rearranged as a modern-day version of a traditional model of social living. So let's think about how we could imagine the life of our communities if the street once again became a space for people's lives, for displaying products in shops, for outdoor tables of bars and restaurants, for public gardens as a meeting place, a natural cushion keeping traffic at a distance and leaving space for human beings.

3.2 From the Conflict "Big Versus Small" to the Dialectic Between Activity and Interactivity

SERVE

15.04.2020_I wait patiently in line outside the local butcher's. A few yards away some women are discussing the pandemic curve in front of the launderette, making the wait even longer. I realise that I have not replied to the shopping group's email in time and I will have to wait until next week. Just as well Valentino from the organic market brought me the meat from his farm in Bore just yesterday. Out of the corner of my eye, I see a shadow approaching from behind. I turn around suddenly, prepared for the worst by the general climate of fear caused by waiting for the peak. A gorgeous blonde ice cream seller smiles at me from behind her mask. Her name is Cecilia. She crossed the street to tell me that if I want, they can deliver ice cream to houses throughout the city. A phone call is all it takes. I thank her for the information and I ask for some immediately—better not put it off and risk forgetting this too. We could really do with something sweet. But in a moment. Right now, I've got to go inside. I can't lose my place in the queue. Of course. No problem. She keeps an eye on me from a distance and, as soon as I come out, she brings over the promised kilo of vanilla, to make sure it wouldn't melt during the wait or, worse still, to make sure I wouldn't go home without it.

As we know, innovative technologies have made huge advances that are increasingly accessible in many areas and their application could have a truly significant impact on people's lives. If we think about it, the potential of digital technology has been apparent in many fields for quite a while. Many local communities were not ready for it, at least until a few months ago. Today everything has changed. The health emergency has been an extraordinary digital trampoline and a powerful training ground for everyone in getting to grips with remote technology. In the space of a few weeks, many of us have gained new abilities and confidence with tools previously not so familiar to everyone. Nearly everyone has become capable of managing a new way of working and social interaction. In fact, we all reacted to being deprived of personal relationships by seizing the new virtual opportunities and the nostalgia for togetherness was matched by the discovery of new ways to communicate remotely.

The memory of physical interaction combined with the necessity for distance created a strange feeling of emotional compensation. Let's think about that for a moment. If we learn a lesson from these two parallel and linked conditions, we can reinvest the positive effects of their synergy into the city of the future. We have all missed the shared work of the past and the contagious enthusiasm of working side by side. We have all learned, however, that we do not always have to be physically present and that it is easy to organise online meetings.

Physical and virtual presence have proved to be complementary and integrable in many situations. Thanks to *lockdown* we can now reassess the importance of spending time in the street while we have also got used to connecting remotely. We are rediscovering the speed, convenience and quality of the corner shop. At the same time, we have also experimented with home delivery and online ordering, perhaps also zero kilometre e-commerce.

From this perspective, centralised urban logistics is now an essential tool to be put in place, which was simply unimaginable just a few months ago. Incentivising it could reduce the continuous traffic of

Fig. 3.2 A. Majoli, *Syracuse. March 15, 2020. Piazza Santa Lucia.* © Photo: Alex Majoli/Magnum

individual couriers and suppliers across the city and allow coordinated distribution of goods and services to be managed remotely.

We have also understood the practicality for the various businesses in a street to be connected and cooperative. Issues such as the commercial theming of streets and coordinating the range of services can finally become a strategic policy and lead to a general rethink of how they fit in to streets and neighbourhoods.

It seems that their social role and commercial significance could be rediscovered. If we think about it, the urgent revival of past practices has been a response to the present situation that can also be taken as a useful lesson for the future. During the difficulties of this period, for example, the practice of home delivery has regained popularity, stimulated by shopkeepers chasing business and by the needs of customers confined in their homes. In the past, this service was normal and was a small but significant contribution to the social bond of the community. We all have some recollection of this. I can still remember as a child, on holidays in the country, waiting for the only event of the morning: the baker on his rounds delivering warm bread and fresh milk around ten o'clock. In my childhood memory, the arrival of the little white van in the gravel lane was to some extent a certainty, a little piece of the emotional stability that I was building and an important sign at that time that I was a small part of something bigger. It wasn't just meeting a friend who cares about you and a chance to break up the long, endless days of the holiday. It was also daily confirmation that there was a larger family than ours in the neighbourhood and a network of relationships we could rely on, no matter.

With the same renewed daily frequency since March, the neighbourhood newsagent has delivered daily newspapers to elderly people isolated in their homes. They have in turn greatly appreciated the deliveries and have looked forward to getting back outside, not least to return the favour and resume the ritual of their morning rounds, bolstered by their gratitude built up over these months for the home delivery service.

We may discover that this resumption of good habits that had been lost will be one of the conditions for survival of the corner shop. Let's hope therefore that the home delivery offered by many shopkeepers during the emergency will stimulate them to recover a relationship with the local customers that was once much more solid.

The drama of today's shops and businesses can become an obligatory transition towards a radical rethink and a more general relaunch, critical not only for the economic strength of the sector but also for the whole community, to the extent that this expansion of business onto public land can interact with people's habits. The so-called *social distancing* to fight infection opens up another extraordinary opportunity on which we can focus. Tourism and culture will have to reorganise their initiatives to follow a similar logic of projection towards the outdoors, attracting entertainment and hospitality into the squares and streets, highlighting a new (but in this case also old) way of using public spaces.

In these areas too, we need to interpret some encouraging signs and reflect on the reminders that pop up in the news. The mayor of Bend, Oregon, has allowed the city's bars and restaurants to occupy car parks outside their premises.[4] The newspaper headline is symptomatic: *Cities in Oregon embrace European-style seating to help restaurants to reopen during the coronavirus crisis*. The American city is adopting the style of the European city and will allow street-facing businesses to expand outdoors in order to meet new health requirements and neutralise the concerns that may keep customers away. The American response to the knock-on crisis in the catering sector is not only an interesting suggestion that could be adopted immediately worldwide. It is also a recognition of value, today more than ever, of the social, commercial and service significance of our public spaces. We can therefore understand that frequenting our streets is an essential part of the relational identity of our cities. The question we need to ask ourselves on this side of the Atlantic is therefore quite predictable. Can the European city remember the *style* that has made it a point of reference throughout the world, its constitutive relationship between the private space and the public space it overlooks, not only as an impromptu solution arising from the emergency but as the restoration of a structural condition for the quality of life of its inhabitants?

The goal of reactivating catering and hospitality businesses can stimulate a forced and worthwhile rethink of the public land they overlook. This will have to involve projecting business owners into the streets, whereas they have in the past often been confined inside their shop fronts due to inappropriate urban design of infrastructure. We can then imagine, plan and share a return to traditional habits by creating a much more lived-in city with a selective logic of routes and traffic. All our movements can then become a personal experience with opportunities for encounters, instead of an obligatory transit to carry out an errand. The selective quality of our movements around the city in the future will

---

[4]https://www.oregonlive.com/dining/2020/05/to-aid-social-distancing-at-restaurants-oregon-cities-embrace-euro-style-street-seating.html.

prevail over the laborious quantity of deliveries being made today. This will provide a new degree of freedom and much more time to recover the social dimension that has been too often neglected in recent years.

We have now understood that this historical quality can be recovered and can work even better. To create a city that reaps the benefits of all these forced experiments means, in fact, accelerating the finalised implementation of the technologies that have now been made available by the *Fourth Industrial Revolution*. Individual journeys can be significantly reduced if we succeed in combining a series of related factors. We will be able to create a system of protected areas where we can move about on foot and by bicycle every day if we can choose to cross a rearranged city that demonstrates a series of related capacities: if the individual businesses on the street make maximum use of the public spaces they overlook, if self-driving vehicles reduce individual multiplication of today's cars by enabling economic and ecological sharing, if centralised logistics reduce journeys to shops, if the willingness of traders to provide home deliveries restores personal relationships and encourages people to return to the shops, and if remote technology removes the need to attend many appointments in person.

If we make the most of all these life conditions, we will combine a return to the habits of a seemingly forgotten past with the intelligent use of technologies that we thought were a thing of the future. We can then imagine a life where we can pick and choose the experiences that interest us. This emergency will have allowed us to rediscover the beauty of living in cities, also through the convenience of delegating tasks that can be performed remotely. Having become aware of the failings that we have suffered and the opportunities that we have enjoyed, this scenario is today considerably closer than yesterday. We can then imagine a situation where the old habits of traditional European city dwellers are enhanced with the new opportunities provided by the permanent interconnection and mandatory digitalisation that we have experienced. The *smart city* can therefore also become a *wise town*.[5] It can enjoy the best conditions of digital accessibility and immediate connections with the world, even in the most isolated districts. At the same time, it can enjoy the particularities and services of a small town, even in the more extensive and undifferentiated contexts.

The health emergency has pushed many towns and cities into rethinking along these lines. For the last few weeks, Paris has been imagining how to re-articulate itself into small centres where everything is at hand and every errand takes 15 min. The French capital, reorganised as a series of *fifteen-minute cities*[6] will have to equip each of these mini environments with schools, parks and shops that can be easily reached on foot and by bicycle. In this case too, Covid 19 encourages radical rethinking of the settlement according to people's needs. From this perspective, the dynamics of regeneration can restart by consolidating distributed local services and fostering neighbourhood units. The existing nuclei could then be the starting point for the recovery of another good habit of old: the model of life tailored to the dimensions of a small town or neighbourhood, but with the general advantages of metropolitan contexts. People's activities and needs could be the nodes around which we weave a new urban mesh of public spaces designed for people, interweaving human relationships and consolidating them over time on this scale. The city can then become intelligent and fast-moving, but also wise and thoughtful. Its inhabitants will be able to choose quality of life over quantity of things to do.

---

[5]Wise city is the first point indicated in *The Monocle Guide to Building Better Cities*, edited by A. TUCK, Gestalten, Berlin 2018.

[6]https://reporterspress.it/universita-sorbonne-il-progetto-per-le-citta-dei-15-minuti-un-ghetto/.

How Human Languages Change

4.1 From the Conflict "Communication Versus Information" to the Truth of Connectivity

UNDERSTAND

22.04.2020_Like every night, once the kids are in bed, I wait with some apprehension for the 10.00 p.m. bulletin with the pandemic data. During the ads, I take a look from my smartphone at the latest video message from Father Mauro connecting, as it were, the Bible to the health emergency, in search of a perspective of salvation. Meanwhile I'm here in front of the screen, but certainly not to listen to generic comments. I'm here, as I am every night, waiting for the links to the experts. I'm hoping to discover something about what lies ahead. I want to know where we are in this nightmare and whether someone can show us a way out. I'm not interested in anything else. Okay. Here we are. Andrea, the professor who took it upon himself in January to supply swabs and reagents for his community, appears via a link from his home. Today he's looking after the entire region. His face is lined like the shutters in the background. He suggests what we should do.

Along with the many suggestions for the city that we have put together, I think it would be interesting to point out another lesson that the health emergency has taught us. I'm thinking how much the ways we communicate and exchange information have changed. Another unexpected advantage, now that everyone has the necessary networking tools, has been the introduction of a new language into everyone's home. After spreading throughout the media, this language is marking the current era and looks like it will be our mental outlook for years to come. One aspect of the last few months we cannot overlook has been the disappearance of superstructures and superimposed communication images. Television programs have been stripped of their predictable sets with their patina of perfection. Live links to experts at home have unleashed the surprising power of what we could previously only imagine as unscheduled cultural incursions. These contributions have now become standard, with all the empathic power of the personal, intimate and unexpected dimension of those taking part. If we think about it, this is a true shift in purpose for television, away from the conventions we were used to. As a result, there will be potential repercussions on how society is influenced through images.

The overall conditions have certainly focussed attention on the content. We will remember this as the period when our need to understand and a great desire for the truth emerged. The need to get to the bottom of things emerged as critical, with unexpected force, marking a clear difference between scientific search for truth and the confusion that surrounded us with a surprising level of

Fig. 4.1 A. MAJOLI, *Palazzolo Acreide. March 15 2020. Man sanitizing the streets.* © Photo: Alex Majoli/Magnum

improvisation. While talk shows were stripped of their audiences and guests, higher-level discussions have proliferated in cultural and scientific contexts, not only on television but also and above on the computer screen. Face to face is undoubtedly still the best format for meetings and discussion, to which we need to return as soon as possible. Nevertheless, we have discovered some more or less obvious facts, for instance that links from home can be easier but also, precisely for this reason, more effective in opening up discussions to many more voices. In doing this we have shown that easy interconnection allows for an exponential multiplication of opportunities for reflection and detailed discussion.

Some understandable prejudices and some automatic habits have disappeared. In the traditional dynamics of information, the duality between truth and connectivity seems to have been completely overturned. The remote has appeared as true because it has been perceived as the search for necessary information at a time of difficulty for everyone. Instead of mere verification, it has been the expectation of an answer that we were all looking for. In the tension of those moments and in the daily need to understand what was happening, all plans were thrown out and every format was improvised. What we saw was what we got, and the reliability of the source became linked day after day to the informality of the discussion. The truth or whatever could be stated about such an unexpected and unfamiliar phenomenon was emerging from doctors' surgeries and hospital wards, from the living rooms or bedrooms of people's homes. The combination of authenticity and remoteness merged into a radically new tone of communication. All this was possible thanks to the wide accessibility of digital interconnection that allowed anyone to connect from anywhere. These links were direct contributions that we would never have enjoyed in a face to face situation, authoritative and long awaited opinions provided through a simple computer connected in an everyday location, without cameras or studio sets, without any filters or hidden agendas. The television studio seemed suddenly trite, a mere support for the actual investigation and search for truth. If we reflect on this experience, we will realise that this outcome is anything but irrelevant and the lesson of remote immediacy is a small intellectual legacy not be wasted.

We are convinced that physical reality will recover its obvious central importance, but it truly be a shame to lose this demonstration of truth that digital technology has given us. We must therefore put this development to good use. This field test has therefore bequeathed us the possibility to reform the purpose of images. The artificial aspects of communication now seem just old and inadequate. A video promoting the restart, a press conference or even an institutional communication are immediately perceived as an implausible performance, as an artificial and empty liturgy. As a result, the perception of the virtual has also been overturned. The immediacy of fact checking has led to a sudden reduction in the irritation of *fake news* and the prejudice of images whose dubious origin needs to be checked. At least for a while, the contribution made by each speaker can no longer be unqualified and merely conventional. It must instead be targeted and essential, both in terms of content and form. We have therefore discovered that we can get closer to the truth through digital technology. It can emerge from open confrontation among opinions of experts who can easily explain to us with competence and simplicity the overall context of the phenomena affecting our lives.

Anti-rhetorical and digital, informal and profound are qualities that have established themselves in a few weeks almost as a standard of communication, closely associated with contemporary information and languages.

Since the beginning of May, the debate on the web has stimulated a reflection among public opinion on the effects of coronavirus in the world of communication, finding consistency between the expectations that the epidemic stimulated and certain trends already in place.[1] For some time now, digital reputation has been a decisive issue in the corporate world: words such as credibility, commitment, participation and sustainability were, in the most advanced contexts, crucial aspects for transparent communication, also with potential significant commercial impact. The severity of the health emergency has made this dynamic an obligatory approach and is forcing the world of business to take a stand on substantial aspects.

The acceleration of these prospects for evolution of productive reality is also reflected immediately on a more general level in information, through the increasingly widespread intellectual reaction to the dynamics of falsification and exploitation that had been taking root for a long time on social media up to the start of the pandemic. For years, there had been a growing need to obtain scientific knowledge and educational information as an instinctive response to the degeneration of the exploitational contrivances that we had tolerated until recently. Now, after everything that has happened, this hope seems to be realised, at least in part, thanks to a new conscious and democratic mobilisation of the network: the sought-after qualities of fairness, trust and consistency have suddenly become conditions for work and knowledge, communication and information.

It seems, therefore, that the search for expertise and the discovery that immediate discussion can be activated over a simple home link are opening up an alternative cultural scenario that is much more pluralistic and informed.

Among the television channels, the inadequacy of previous conventions has seemed immediately outmoded, to the point of becoming ridiculous. This sea change was immediately apparent. The

---

[1]See, for example, the dedicated articles from wired.it and design@large.it, widely available on social media.

selection of guests, the sobriety of the contributions, the domesticity of the images, as well as the dramatic nature of the events, have made us all re-appreciate the necessity of accurate information and the associated need for high-level thinking combined with a direct and informal approach.

It is not only content that has been stripped back to the essentials. The mode of communication has followed this emotional tension, demonstrating the practicality of technological confidence, indelibly marking the image of these opening months of the 2020s. It will perhaps continue to mark the coming years, if we manage to cultivate, grow and consolidate this cultural conquest of truth which, if we think about it, is adopting the humility and willingness to debate typical of research.

4.2 From the Conflict "Form Versus Substance" to the Frugality of Contemporaneity

THRIVE

29.04.2020_For weeks I've been taking turns with my sister to do the shopping, going out as little as possible and leaving our parents locked up at home. We hadn't shared duties for a long time, of which food is perhaps the most pleasant one. Andrea has proved better than us. With volunteers from the neighbourhood, he cycles back and forth between houses and shops, making deliveries to the elderly. Elena and Renato are at the hospital day and night. They have put their lives on hold. They sleep separated from their family and haven't seen the children for weeks. They are battling through the crisis alongside the other doctors and nurses. The peak of the wave has passed but it is still dropping very slowly. I think about them a lot. From time to time, I call them, listen to them, and encourage them.

Rediscovery of the truth, also through digital connectivity, has triggered a different style of cultural approach with potentially very positive effects that we can only guess for now. We reached 2020 in an intellectual torpor, from which it has been difficult to rouse ourselves, lounging on inherited inertia, allowing formerly antagonistic attitudes to coexist in indifference, in a great confusion of orientations that denied the possibility of sharing a common cultural perspective and without being able to imagine the prospect of rekindling conversations that are now more necessary than ever. The Covid-19 emergency and the risk to life have given us an opportunity (perhaps even forced us) to assume a position and to halt the indifferent proliferation of the languages we were using.

The postmodern dimension that we have seen continue until yesterday, along with the excesses and divisions to which we had become accustomed, seems to have been definitively abandoned in favour of a radical search for essentiality. A restart on these foundations of informal and spontaneous, pluralistic and digital truth could suggest a new intellectual dimension and a new overall aesthetic outlook that could greatly influence artistic, literary, cultural, as well as architectural and urban developments. Moreover, I think it could also reintroduce a sense of authenticity to the communication that surrounds us. The debate that has already been ongoing for some time in many fields of thought on what direction our actions should take is now emerging in all its importance, with interesting repercussions also in the context of cities. Pope Francis' invitation to take up the *challenge to urban cultures*, with the aim of unveiling the spirituality of places in order to relaunch a possible redemption of the suburbs, starting by exploiting their spontaneous feelings, opens up a cultural revolution that is already being felt. In the philosophical arena, the phenomenological and existential approach is returning centre stage through its architectural and urban impacts, with the *critique of aesthetic capitalism*[2] and a reflection that challenges ethics and politics on the issues of sharing,

---

[2]G. BÖME, *Critique of Aesthetic capitalism,* Mimesis International, Milan 2017.

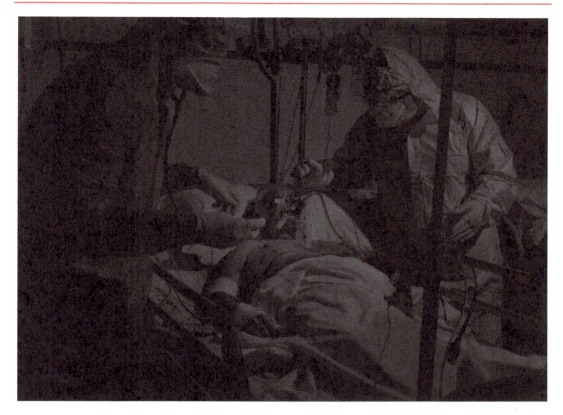

Fig. 4.2 A. MAJOLI, *Italy, Catania. Sicily. March 25, 2020. In the intensive care unit of the Canizzaro hospital a man with coronavirus is made to breathe with the help of a ventilator.* © Photo: Alex Majoli/Magnum

coexistence and, consequently, living.³ In the same way, the reflections of political, social and economic disciplines on the civil significance of human experience may reason about the real needs of our communities and refocus attention on people and how they live together. From this perspective, the word *responsibility*—in the sense of taking care of something—was already reassuming a central role among established businesses as part of a special commitment to so-called *corporate social responsibility*.⁴ In the meantime, the theme of *Community Governance* has become pivotal in the context of supporting civil commitment and rationalising action in organisational terms and in institutional relations once again around principles like social responsibility and sustainability.⁵ Much has already been said in these fields too. Much was already primed for a restart that would reorganise the fundamental issues. Much was already oriented towards a new attitude, to take an extreme example, also in the areas more closely linked to consumption. This is the case with *Marketing 4.0*, which has for some years now focused on the central role of trust and transparency, customer relationships and the importance of service.⁶ To touch briefly on the realm of architecture, which concerns me directly, we just need to refocus on the increasingly urgent goal of relaunching the spirit of the Modern Movement as a sensitive and progressive investigation into the purpose of what we do

---

³For the Italian debate on these issues see *I luoghi e gli altri, la cura dell'abitare*, edited by C. DANANI, Aracne Rome 2016.
⁴S. ZAMAGNI, *Responsabili, come civilizzare il mercato*, Il Mulino Bologna 2019.
⁵F. MANFREDI, *Community governance, Comunità in azione*, Cacucci Editore Bari 2013.
⁶P. KOTLER, H. KARTAJAYA and I. SETIAWAN, *Marketing 4.0. Dal tradizionale al digitale*, Hoepli Milan 2017.

and ensure that practice of the project regains the meaning of a responsible response, that *necessary possible* recently suggested by the late Vittorio Gregotti.[7]

Today, in the wake of the coronavirus, we cannot hide any longer. Frugality could be the outcome of the coming period, if we can recover its original meaning—more positive, broader and more universal than we might imagine.

As often happens, much of the deeper meaning of concepts is hidden in the etymological origin of the term. For the Romans, frugality was a value, a habit that became an adaptation. In Latin, *Frugalitas* is in no way linked to the concept of deprivation. *Frugalitas* is instead linked to the adjective *frugi*, meaning useful, which is in turn derived from the noun *frux*, fruit. At its origin, therefore, frugality did not mean renunciation but instead the proposition of an action with a purpose, the identification and achievement of a goal, the operational predisposition that favours the result. For centuries, *frugality* was the norm for people everywhere. However, with the beginning of the twentieth century it became one of the many victims of *consumer engineering* linked to the rise of modern technology, despite the many attempts at resistance that we have briefly mentioned. Those dynamics that have persisted up to the present, at the end of a process of continuous implementation, have now been put on hold by the health emergency and the unprecedented economic crisis that has followed it. In the same direction, this shock and interruption can therefore be the cultural opportunity for a restart following new routes that were actually traced out a long time ago.

Frugality today, after such a difficult and exceptional situation, means a return to the discipline of awareness, that *tacit knowledge* as a *Darwinian concept* of adaptability to rapidly changing scenarios of which the psychologist Paolo Legrenzi speaks.[8] The studies he mentions point to the importance of leaving room for the unexpected. They demonstrate that setting oneself a more important objective (or finding oneself having to accept it) transforms today's sacrifice into a conscious step towards a more balanced condition and the promise of a better life. The frugal perspective that is emerging from many quarters as a valued approach appears, however, an unlikely prospect without a widespread individual reflection that can mobilise collective sentiment, perhaps based on the experience of the pandemic.[9]

Many of the issues that are being discussed today—the fight against climate change, resilience, energy transitions, the shift of meaning from possession to use across many areas, starting with means of transport—can, if we think about it, be linked back to this concept. Frugality means in fact choosing solidity and *anti-fragility*. In the final analysis, it means seeking the essential.

If we can manage to follow this direction in all fields, frugality can therefore be a motif for our times and simultaneously a guarantee of value. Substance for form or, more precisely, the form of substance can become the shared centre of the world of relationships that we could easily activate, with a new awareness, remotely too. We will then be able to restart from a *culture of the technical* that has yet to be discussed, from a new critical modernity detached from the dynamics imposed by consumption, from a present understood as a lucid and sensitive immersion in the challenges of the contemporary world, as a bold confrontation with the dramatic conditions we are experiencing and with the vast potential we have before us. Perhaps it would be natural to start again from some basic concepts that primarily affect our individual responsibilities, such as the one professed by Ernesto Nathan Rogers when he wrote, concerning the architect's profession, that *even if we pursue the method, the only guarantee is the ethical yardstick of poetics.*[10]

---

[7]V. GREGOTTI, *Il possibile necessario*, Bompiani Milan 2014.

[8]P. LEGRENZI, *Frugalità*, Il Mulino Bologna 2014, p. 25.

[9]This theme is the focus of the introduction of E. WASTACOTT, *Frugalità, Storie della vita semplice*, Luiss University Press, Rome 2017.

[10]E. N. ROGERS, *Esperienza d'architettura,* Einaudi, Turin 1958. This sentence can be found in the conclusion to the introductory essay *Il mestiere dell'architetto.*

How Improve Our Real-World Settings

5.1 From the Conflict "Development Versus Form" to the Forward Thinking Starting from the Settlement Reality

CHANGE

06.05.2020 _ During these long days of reflection on the city, I am thinking again of how many signs had already been evident for a long time. I think back to how people everywhere had already indicated what they wanted through their behaviour. I think of the urgent need to rediscover the ability to listen. I think of what administrators and citizens have told me in recent years. I think back to the meetings with Maria, Alessandro and the whole council to discuss the system of places and public parks for the Formigine Strategic Urban Project. Agata recalled how the residents of her hamlet gather every weekend to walk the few kilometres to the regional capital, along the narrow banks of the winding stream that cuts through the countryside. Alfonso was recently telling me how in Andria they have surprisingly pedestrianised a quadrilateral of roads just outside the historical centre. One day the water pipe broke and the road flooded. When it was reopened, after months of closure for works that were never carried out, there was uproar among both traders and inhabitants who had become used to living without cars and to meeting up every evening for an aperitif. I remember that in Sorbolo, Nicola was not sure why the Town Plan envisaged a road junction to connect the neighbourhood on the other side of the railway to the provincial road. He was pleased when we showed him that for about half the cost they could connect it directly to the town square with an urban passageway designed as a subterranean garden, resolving the isolation of that part of town, the problem of smog and the dangers of the level crossing in one fell swoop. The people of the village understood. The project is now under way and the Plan will be adjusted. The bulldozers will soon move in.

One critical conflict that must be overcome concerns the separation between the constructed settlement and the instruments of its governance.

The results are plain to see in the difference between the acknowledged quality of the historical city and the widespread lack of quality in the suburbs. This difference can only be bridged with great patience by overcoming the dimension of indeterminacy and the loss of meaning of the most recent settlement, in some ways attributable to the negative definition of *non-place*.[1] The ethnographer and

---

[1] This neologism was coined by Marc Augé in 1992. See M. AUGÉ, *Non luoghi, Introduzione a un'antropologia della surmodernità*, Elèuthera, Milan 2005. It is discussed in D. COSTI, *Non-luogo*, entry in *Enciclopedia dell'architettura* edited by A. DE POLI, Motta architettura, Milan 2008.

Fig. 5.1 A. MAJOLI, *Italy, Catania. March 19, 2020. Street scene.* © Photo: Alex Majoli/Magnum

anthropologist Marc Augé famously used this term a few years ago to indicate the indifferent space produced by the impersonal and overly rapid transformation brought about by globalisation. This identitary, relational and historical failing can also be found, on a larger scale, in dealing with settlements. It is the outcome of accelerated growth, which needs more sedimentation, more time and progressive social recognition. We must therefore create the conditions to begin at least that partial recovery of purpose for the peripheries that Augé has been hoping for recently. The expectation of *what there will be one day*[2] of which he speaks, adjusting the focus to some extent away from the initial definition, leaves the prospect open for a progressive attribution of value and increased affinity with the people, to be pursued over time. We know, on the other hand, together with philosopher Jean Luc Nancy, that the city is a permanently evolving living organism, it is *restless heart, clearing and invasion*, always a temporary completion consisting of continuous movements and transformations.[3]

From this perspective of progressive and continuous refinement, we are faced with the responsibility of dealing with a very particular moment in history, and not only because of the health emergency. The continuous growth that has resulted in the uncontrolled expansion of most Italian cities and many European cities since World War II has now come to a halt, triggering the greatest urban crisis of the last hundred years. I often recall that the plans of the individual local authorities in Emilia Romagna up to 2010, before the start of the obligatory era of *Zero Land Consumption* and *Urban Regeneration*, covered three and a half times the current extent of the Bologna metropolitan

---

[2]M. AUGE, *Rovine e macerie, il senso del tempo*, Bollati Boringhieri Turin 2004.
[3]J. L. NANCY, *La città lontana*, Ombre Corte, Verona 2002.

area.[4] Against this projection, which would have definitively compromised the settlement structure of the cities and the qualities of the surrounding landscape, reality has proved so far removed from urban planning forecasts that they have been declared a substantial failure.

Here too, then, a change of approach appears necessary for urban transformation governance instruments, not only because of the failings that we have noted but also because of the much more distinctly architectural issues that we need to address. In fact, today we are tasked with thinking about how to reorganise the constructed urban fabric and the vacant land available at the end of a lengthy phase that has often overlooked quality in its frenetic growth. Therefore, it is going to take some patience and a lot of fieldwork to achieve an acceptable configuration. In the meantime, the periphery can be adapted, and then reorganised and improved year on year through an overall review of the collective space and afterwards, on a much longer time scale, a system can be agreed on that may seem definitive but will in any case always be in progress. While the substantial modification of the city where we live can exploit the virtual and connective dimension as its chief ally in resuming the substance of the old discussions, we will still have to concentrate our efforts in the coming years on one last very concrete operational, real and verifiable issue: the guiding of urban regeneration through architecture and transforming this rediscovery into a rule.

I use the term rediscovery because it was like this until just a few decades ago. This change of approach is in fact nothing new. It is actually a return to the past. While not forgetting that the architectural project has generally always been the instrument for changing the city, this new situation is an exemplary episode of how a health issue can become an opportunity for urban improvement and drive the intervention methodology and legislation forward.

A story very similar to the one we have experienced in recent months is described in the social novel *Il ventre di Napoli* [The Bowels of Naples], which deals with cholera in that city in the second half of the nineteenth century.[5] After a continuous series of epidemics, some parts of the old city were demolished. They were considered unhealthy because they were too densely built for settlement to be reorganised according to hygienic criteria of thinning with adequate sewerage infrastructure. This renovation work set the direction of urban policy that continued for decades, but not without negative effects, underhand speculation, evident limitations to the respect for historical and artistic heritage and the lack of quality of many interventions. Besides these considerations, the importance of that reaction and the determination of a response that actually managed to become law should be recognised. It initiated a regulatory debate of great importance that was highly innovative for the time. It is therefore worth dwelling on the structural results of that dramatic experience. At that time, the health emergency stimulated a practical intervention—*gutting*—with the redesigning of entire districts, not only in Naples but in many Italian cities. From this background emerged the *Law of Naples*, a decisive development in national legislation on these issues. We know that urban hygiene is, for this very reason, one of the cornerstones of modern urban planning. However, it is also an issue that has regained increasing importance over recent years and has now assumed a central role in the face of the global dimension of conflicts between urbanisation and health.[6]

Admittedly, conditions are very different today. While the city was the problem back then, today it may be the solution. The lesson that we can take from this therefore touches on two issues raised by health problems of a similar magnitude more than a hundred years ago: the extraordinary intervention

---

[4]This value was presented at the Conference *Il Consumo di suolo in Emilia-Romagna analisi dello stato di fatto* [Land Consumption in Emilia-Romagna: analysis of the state of affairs] in October 2015 as the result of a census on planning carried out jointly by the Urban Planning and Agriculture Departments of the Emilia Romagna Region.

[5]M. SERAO, *Il ventre di Napoli*, Treves, Milan 1884.

[6]M. C. TREU, *Città, salute, sicurezza. Strumenti di governo e casi di studio—La gestione del rischio*, Maggioli, San Arcangelo di Romagna (RM) 2009.

based on new approaches to the organisation of the settled space and the translation of this urban renewal into rules through legislation. Despite some differences, those events are still operationally topical. A memory remains of a reaction that produced structured rather than episodic results: today too, the manner of intervention—certainly on a smaller scale and with much more controlled impacts—must be concretely tested and the prospect of the regulatory stabilisation of solutions must be initiated and discussed from the outset.

The last dialectic that must be reactivated is therefore that of the relationship that had vanished for decades between reality and project on the urban scale. The goal we need to pursue is to bring architecture back within planning instruments, using it not only as the final stage of implementation but also as an initial space to put forward a vision of the city to be shared with the population.

Today the crucial theme for the contemporary city is to think about the possibility of configuring it in a different way, starting first of all from the object of interest. Urban Design must focus on empty rather than full spaces, on the availability of free space rather than on building capacity, and on reorganisation rather than expansion of suburban settlement. If we realise that the historic city is the gradual outcome of a selection that has lasted more than two thousand years, we will not be surprised to discover that the expansion achieved from the post-war period to the present is nothing more than an approach to settlement and that the efforts required of us in the coming decades will have to focus on its continuous and collective modification. Let us not forget, however, that the response we must give is to develop a system of public places through cities as an alternative setting for slow mobility and, at the same time, as an opportunity for renewed sociality. The centre of our attention must therefore be the urban land that we can connect, the interstices—that *intermediate space* of the cities we are always talking about—the *fragile landscapes*[7] to be rearranged as a coordinated set of public spaces. Only through stitching vacant land together intelligently will we be able to recreate the physical conditions for rebuilding the communities settled there. Around the central objective of connecting parks and available areas to form a system of places for slow mobility and sociality we can articulate a series of related strategies: those prompted by the concentration of services to integrate the existing ones, those of settlement densification and property development of the urbanised context that must, in the interest of all concerned, be interwoven with the overall and strategic regeneration of neighbourhoods.

The challenge for the city during and after Covid-19 is to build on what we have learned and to exploit what we have rediscovered also from this point of view, taking the opportunity of continued *social distancing* to rebuild the settlement structures around people, combining the series of objectives we have discussed so far into a single integrated strategy: rethink the design of public spaces also as an urban projection of high street businesses; promote the use of bicycles to renew and complete a system of public places and parks as an alternative to the road network; exploit the potential of interconnected digital technology to make better use of our time and to reimagine individual and collective living spaces with more flexible approaches and for more varied uses; reorganise neighbourhoods and stimulate the establishment of services that can grow around the new dynamics that may be activated.

All these issues must be brought together quickly into a truly workable synthesis, case by case and city by city. The overall logic of the interventions to be arranged as soon as possible and to be developed in the next few years must be based on the particularities of each case. This specificity must also and above all be a reference point in searching for a new way of recomposing traditional functions, combining public interest and private initiative, in line with the objectives and needs of contemporary society.

---

[7]The theme of urban land to be recovered and fragile landscapes is a highly topical issue in research. See *Paesaggi fragili*, edited by G. BERTELLI, Aracne Editrice, Rome 2018.

On this basis, we will therefore have to reassert the importance of two suspended mutual relationships that need to be recovered: those between architecture and city and between project and service.

The former will have to overcome current self-referentiality and re-establish the former physiological relationship. We continue to believe in a principle that may seem obvious but which in reality appears to have been forgotten. We still think that architecture and cities are necessary to each other. We must therefore reassert the need for architecture to find much of its rationale in the city, and for the city to rediscover architecture as its conscious construction. If we do this, architecture can once again become the most effective response to the needs of the city.

The second mutual relationship concerns the approach of the actions we can implement. The instrument for implementing all the *ideas of cities* made urgent by Covid 19 can therefore no longer be the same as that adopted in the past for an expanding city and which clearly failed the predictions no more than ten years ago. I'm obviously not contemplating a meaningless and time-worn battle between Plan and Project. I am thinking instead of an alliance between the qualities of analysis and governance of the former and the investigative and foresight capabilities of the latter. In the interest of urban planning too, the answer could be provided by the Urban Project, conceived strategically as an oriented process of construction of preliminary architectural scenarios to be shared with the population. The characteristics of concreteness and immediate practicality that it guarantees, together with the knowledge skills that it contributes and with the active participation of the population that it manages to stimulate, point to resumption of the traditional instrument for change. Only a formal preview of the possible changes can transform the vision of the future city into a collective challenge. If planning alone is no longer sufficient, however, the project will also require a new approach of community service. From this perspective, it must avoid the temptation of complacency, however legitimate, of its objectual or sculptural characterisation and must reimagine itself in a renewed civil dimension. It must then be put forward as an interpretative synthesis of the answers to people's needs by gathering together the precious contributions of innovative technologies and all the disciplines that can immediately improve the cities where we live, that are today capable of becoming smart (rapid and reflective at the same time) and sustainable.[8]

This is the only way that we will be able to pursue the *affective city*[9] that we will be able to appraise depending on the extent to which its citizens recognise its value and on the feeling that all the spaces designed to welcome them can stimulate.

5.2 From the Conflict "Governance Versus Commitment" to the Emulative Dialectic Between Private and Public

ACT

**13.05.2020 _ *Phase 2 seems to be going well. In the city, infection rates are dropping day after day. For some time now, we've been thinking about how to restart. It looks like this problem is going to persist for some time. I ask Gabriele, who is studying the virus, how long we'll have to wait to get back to our old lives. He tells me the problem won't be solved any time soon. He tells me they still don't know enough about it. The emergency will last until a vaccine is found. We are going to be in*

---

[8]On these themes, following research carried out over the last few years, I am currently finishing the Strategic Urban Design Manual, which will be released in late 2021. See D. COSTI, *Urban Strategic Design, architecture for the smart and wise city 4.0,* part of the Series *The City Project*, Springer Berlin, currently being printed.

[9]Regarding this concept, see the reflection in the chapter *La città affettiva* in F. DE MATTEIS, *Vita nello spazio, sull'esperienza affettiva dell'architettura*, Mimesis Milan-Udine, 2019 pp. 139–152.

Fig. 5.2 A. MAJOLI, *Italy, Catania, March 14, 2020. Street shop near the port.* © Photo: Alex Majoli/Magnum

this situation perhaps for another year, and it might come back sooner or later in another form. We might have to live indefinitely with the risk of global infection and social distancing. Emanuele reminds me about the afternoon appointment with the undergraduates. We need to check the latest fine-tuning of the cycle/pedestrian system of parks and public spaces in Modena. Andrea prepares the proposal for integrated pilot projects for the Region. He arranges an online meeting for Thursday with Francesco, Paolo and Marko, who are working on self-driving transport at another university. Davide writes to me to promote an urban scenario of carbon neutrality by 2030. The solutions are already available. They need to be put together and tested. Is this perhaps the perfect time to fix our contemporary cities?

The emotion and worry of this period seem capable of speeding up recent dynamics that were already greatly accelerated. They have firmly established a need for intervention that now seems unavoidable and have made systemic mobilisation urgent.

In a recent reflection, the constitutional expert Sabino Cassese asserts that we can no longer consider Democracy as a given or as a conquest achieved for all time, and he identifies civil society as its main defence against power.[10] Therefore, it is not politics or institutions but people in their collective dimension who undertake this delicate but crucial task. While the Italian Constitution calls upon all citizens to take an interest, in reality we reached 2020 with a discordant feeling that has consolidated an attitude of intolerance (and in some cases anger) among the population, in which a rejection of commitment and the demand to be heard coexist to a large degree. In this case too, the

---

[10]S. CASSESE, *La democrazia e i suoi limiti*, Mondadori Milan 2017.

trauma of Covid-19 may represent a new start. Perhaps today, in light of what has happened, this distance can be bridged, at least in part, and the conflict between government and community can be reconciled. Cassese also points out some very recent encouraging signs: participation, albeit passive, in the political life of the country, a public debate that is still feasible and the spontaneous activation of grassroots movements.[11] Perhaps confidence will be restored in a relationship—too often characterised by disappointment—between politicians and citizens by working on these fundamentals and radically changing the register of relationships: by systematically practising *Deliberative Democracy* in Southern Europe too, by activating real forums of debate, as Urban Centers and local agencies should be,[12] and by initiating transparent processes for sharing strategic choices with communities and for cities.

Civil Society will be the primary contributor in this debate, if it is recognised for its value as the point of contact with people, as a *membrane*, according to the definition of the sociologist Mauro Magatti,[13] that allows the vital osmosis between individuals and institutions. The growth in the role of the voluntary sector therefore opens up an important space for exchange (and an equally necessary opportunity for reciprocation), which can be supported by recognition of the increasingly significant role that it demonstrates not only as a social glue but also as an economic reality.[14]

In reality, today much more so than before, individuals are ahead the institutions.

If the country's political class understands this situation, it will be able make the most of a situation in which the non-profit and private sectors clearly outstrip the public sector in terms of initiative and capacity for action. This is why the voluntary sector and business have for several years been leading the transition towards a new model of responsible, collaborative and sustainable development, pushing forward a change of system that must absolutely be encouraged and supported.

In Italy, since about 2016, things seemed to have been freed up and to be moving ever more quickly towards common goals through the increasingly solid construction of networks of stakeholders who have mobilised in many areas. In recent times, a collective sensitivity to the issues of civil commitment and the environment has acquired a whole new consistency and determination. Some examples point to a new dynamism and a marked attitude of independence, with the substantial transformation of the public sector from subject of policies to an object under pressure to follow them, or at least not to slow them down. A number of cases are symptomatic of this change. In 2016 the *Alliance for Sustainable Development* was founded, which brings together associations, universities and research centres committed to the implementation of UN Agenda 2030 for sustainable development. Its activity encourages and puts pressure on the public sector. Among various initiatives, it pushes the Government and the Public Administrations to implement actions: each year it draws up a report on how the country is working towards the goals that have been set, it intervenes in lawmaking, it engages with Ministries in order to speed up policy and to offset accumulated delays.[15]

---

[11]S. Cassese, *Il buon governo. L'età dei doveri*, Mondadori Milan 2020.

[12]We may note international mobilisation in this regard with the activation of EUCANET, the *European Agencies Network for citizenship, inclusion, involvement and empowerment of communities through the urban transformation process*. https://eucanet.wordpress.com/.

[13]M. Magatti, *Il potere istituente della società civile*, Laterza Rome-Bari 2005.

[14]Law 106 of 2016 reorganises previous legislation with the definition of the *Third Sector as the set of private entities established for civic, solidarity and social utility purposes that, on a non-profit basis, promote and carry out activities of general interest, through forms of voluntary and free action or mutual benefit or production and exchange of goods and services, in accordance with the purposes established in their respective statutes or deeds of incorporation.*

[15]On 25 September 2015, the United Nations approved Agenda 2030 for sustainable development and the corresponding 17 Sustainable Development Goals (*Sustainable Development Goals*—SDG). On 3 February 2016, the *ASVIS Alliance for Sustainable Development* was founded by the Unipolis Foundation and the "Tor Vergata" University of Rome (see https://asvis.it). An analytical reflection on these issues is contained in E. Giovannini, *L'utopia sostenibile*, Editori Laterza Bari Rome, 2018.

Reflection on the circular economy is increasingly becoming a strategic thinking resource for the transition to a business model that has to deal with the crisis. With growing global awareness, a private organisation, the *Ellen McArthur Foundation*, is committed to demonstrating the economic potential of this systemic shift by involving multinational companies, businesses and project research centres in an extensive network of members and partners around the world.[16] In fact, in the middle of lockdown an interview with its founder was released in which she assured the success of this transformation precisely because of its spontaneous nature, precisely because it will come from the grassroots through the mobilisation of a multitude of stakeholders: *We are talking about total, far-reaching and positive change. There are so many people rushing in this direction. The time will come when there will be no way of stopping them.*[17] The age of urban regeneration, which is slowly gathering pace, is therefore overlapping with the era of the *3 Rs—Re-use, Repair, Reproduction—* which seems capable of mobilising society and redirecting the investments of economic operators, with important repercussions on the environment.[18]

In this same direction, in the industrial field, some recent signs can be interpreted as strategic indicators that see the private sector leading the public sector in outlining and supporting a clear vision of the future. The most sensitive and informed companies are exercising their *Corporate Social Responsibility* through a series of increasingly coordinated actions. In Italy, the economy, as part of its civil dimension, has increasingly opened up in recent years to sustainable development and to the local territory.[19] Every month, more and more companies sign up to the *BCorp* certified protocol aimed at *using business as a positive force*, building an increasingly broad and global collaborative network of players. The individual perspective can thus become part of a collective action aimed at giving a new meaning to private employment and promoting a change in the system that also involves the public sector. This contagious phenomenon is also spreading in the global context with exponential growth in just the last few years, demonstrating its importance in this situation.[20] During lockdown, Italian BCorp companies promoted the *#UnlocktheChange* initiative, calling for a radical change with an appeal to institutions to opt for interdependence and sustainability. Here again we see the private sector asking the public sector to follow its lead, not to slow the momentum and to unleash the transformation of country.[21]

This health emergency has therefore highlighted the importance of a permanent presence of such organisations, of this *strategic philanthropy* of the private sector that has arisen from the emergency situation and carries out a constant structured action across the territory.[22] It will come as no surprise then to discover that in Italy, while Covid-19 was having its worst impact, a long list of players from civil society and the business world signed a manifesto for a *Green New Deal*.[23] The document calls

---

[16] The Ellen McArthur Private Foundation promotes the transition from a linear to a circular economy https://www.ellenmacarthurfoundation.org.

[17] This is the last sentence in the interview with Ellen McArthur, which appeared in the press and was picked up by the Internet on 28.03.2020. See https://www.designatlarge.it/ellen-macarthur-intervista/.

[18] W. R. STAHEL, *The Circular Economy—A User Guide*, Routledge, London 2019.

[19] L. BECCHETTI, L. BRUNI and S. ZAMAGNI, *Economia civile e sviluppo sostenibile. Progettare e misurare un nuovo modello di benessere*, Ecra, Rome 2019.

[20] 2016 also saw the publication of the Italian translation of the book on *BCorps*, R. HONEYMAN, *Il manuale della B Corp. Usare il Business come Forza Positiva* [*The B Corp Handbook: How You Can Use Business as a Force for Good*], Bookabook Milan 2016.

[21] See *Unlockthechange.it* and https://www.ilsole24ore.com/art/appello-bcorp-imprese-e-istituzioni-scegliete-ora-sostenibilita-ADBmfBd.

[22] https://secondowelfare.it/terzo-settore/fondazioni/zamagni-la-filantropia-deve-uscire-da-una-logica-emergenziale-e-adottare-un-approccio-strategico.html.

[23] The Manifesto *Uscire dalla pandemia con un nuovo green deal per l'Italia* [*Emerging from the pandemic with a new green deal for Italy*] was presented on 7 May 2020 and broadcast on social networks under #greendealitalia.

for the *European Recovery Plan* to be oriented towards certain objectives: quality production, circular economy, energy transition to a climate neutral economy, sustainable agriculture, urban regeneration, natural capital, carbon-free mobility and digital innovation.

These same domains have provided the stimulus and support to promote cultural and environmental policies to develop the territory. One case in my city is symptomatic of the independent mobilisation of support and incentive. Again since 2016, in Parma the association of citizens and companies *Parma io ci sto!* ['Parma count me in!'] has been supporting the institutions and promoting a series of virtuous actions, including the successful candidacy of *Parma Italian Capital of Culture*, participation in the *Green Capital Award*, the creation of the *Green Kilometer* as an environmental buffer belt for fine particles running alongside the motorway, and the plan for *Carbon Neutrality* by 2030, which is now being implemented.[24]

Public bodies and the city are completely unprepared to face these revolutionary but concrete prospects, which were simply unimaginable until a few years ago. In this very recent but very intense flow of actions that imply a cultural re-founding of processes and a radical reorganisation of society, it is therefore urgent to redefine the relationship between public political responsibility and pioneering private projects. Within this extraordinary period of transition through which we are living, a realignment of the instruments for governance of urban transformations that are still awaiting truly incisive methods of intervention and convincing ways of involving the population would appear to be crucial. On this basis, it is in fact possible today to explore how to reorganise the contemporary city and verify its immediate viability.

This will require a broad vision and steady grip. The issue of governance of urban transformation will have to take these new complexities into account and interpret this accelerated dynamic through increasingly interdisciplinary and genuinely effective tools for synthesis. We insist that the Strategic Urban Project be transposed by urban planning legislation as the preliminary part of the initial planning document. We welcome the first voluntary and experimental applications among Agencies[25] that are today launching urban regeneration with integrated scenarios in which the population has a stake. We propose that the architectural design of public spaces be the tool to implement a *smart and wise city*, reorganising the public city around people, organising urban parks and vacant land, and taking advantage of the technological innovations of the *fourth industrial revolution* that will make it possible to create a city that is smart but also wise, and of *big data* as well as critical reflection: the *City of Man* 4.0.

If the response is adequate, it will perhaps be possible to resolve one final conflict—the one between government and community, between policies and projects, between pretending and doing. The resurgence of an emulative dialectic of recovery between public and private sectors is the engine that can transform the primarily cultural fabric of society and steer a transformation of the physical structure of its cities, with efficient integrated tools and according to new values that rediscover ancient principles.

Now is the time.

---

[24]In Parma since 2016, the *Parma io ci sto!* Association has been promoting initiatives to support and guide urban and territorial policies on 5 areas of interest: Agrifood, Culture, Tourism and Leisure, Training and Innovation, and Environmental Sustainability. See https://www.parmaiocisto.com/.

[25]We have for some years been working to support the Agencies and Public Administration on these issues. The *Strategic Urban Plans* for Sorbolo, Mezzani, Albareto, Formigine and Carpi will be included in the upcoming urban planning instruments that are currently being launched. At the same time, the Municipality of Molfetta has adopted this methodology as the working basis for the Plan currently being drawn up.

9783030761028